Mrs. Mayo's

Book of Creative Foods:

A Complete Guide to Fancy Food Decorating <u>Anyone</u> Can Do

Written and Illustrated

By

ESTHER MURPHY

Mrs. Mayo's
Book of Creative Foods:
A Complete Guide to Fancy Food Decorating **Anyone** Can Do

BY ESTHER MURPHY

All rights reserved. No part of this publication may be reproduced or transmitted in any form or by any means, electronic or mechanical, including photocopy, recording (audio or video) or any information storage and retrieval system, without permission from the publisher.

Reviewers who would like to include brief quotations in newspapers, magazines, newsletters or other legitimate forms of communication, audio or video, need not seek the publisher's permission.

Copyright © 1983 by Deco-Press Publishing Co.
First Edition

Printed in the United States of America

Published by
Deco-Press Publishing Co.
P.O. Box 29489
Denver, Colorado 80229

Library of Congress Cataloging in Publication Data

Murphy, Esther.
   Mrs. Mayo's Book of creative foods.

  1. Cookery (Garnishes) 2. Food presentation.
I. Title. II. Title: Book of creative foods.
TX652.M865   1983   641.5   83-11546
ISBN 0-937016-01-2

TABLE OF CONTENTS

	Introduction	5
	Author's Preface	9
I	Vegetable Artistry	11

    Carving vegetable flowers for Centerpieces and Relish Dishes.

II	Appetizers	21

    Decorated Canapes, hot & cold Hors d'Oeuvres and savory Dips.

III	Party Snacks in Decorative Shapes	43

    Cheese Balls, Logs and other decorative shapes.

IV	Tea Sandwiches	51

    Pinwheels, Mosaics, Checkerboards, Ribbons, and much more.

V	Gelatine Salads & Aspics	63

    Fashioning designs with vegetables and meats.

VI	Party Sandwich Loaves	73

    Savory fillings inside...frosted with cream cheese and decorated with Flowers and Horn of Plenty with Vegetables.

| VII | Chaud Froid Buffet Molds | 85 |

Fancy meat molds, covered with a rich, creamed gelatine sauce and decorated for various occasions, including holidays.

| VIII | Desserts | 101 |

Miniature Pastries, decorated Gelatine Molds, Bavarian Creams, Petits Fours and Icing Recipes.

Summer Coating — 121

Make delicious candies, mints and holiday molds the easy way!

Marzipan — 129

All about making those delightful miniature fruits and vegetables with marzipan.

| IX | Punches | 147 |

A variety of recipes and the "how to" of making a decorative Ice Piece for the punch bowl!

| X | "Meat & Potatoes" | 153 |

Just <u>good food</u> made attractive with a minimum of effort!

| XI | Menus | 161 |
| XII | Servings Per Person | 165 |

There's Money in Catering and Decorating — 169

About the Author — 175

INTRODUCTION

How many times have you begun planning a festive occasion only to wish there was something more to serve than crackers, cheese & dip or sliced meat, potato salad and deviled eggs?

How many times have you wished you were something more than a "parsley and paprika" food decorator? And that you could be creative (and appreciated) without having to spend a lot of money for equipment and training?

If so, then this book is for you! Whether you're planning a simple birthday party for the children, a cocktail party for the boss or to celebrate a professional promotion, a holiday reception to toast goodtimes, or simply a neighborhood get-together.... you'll find dozens and dozens of ways to make your food "sparkle" with time-saving methods.

For the first time, and in one publication, here is a book containing everything you always wanted to know about Fancy Food Decorating and Party Catering (but didn't know where to look or who to ask!).

The publication is the result of numerous requests by present and former students of the MRS. MAYO'S SCHOOL of CAKE DECORATING for information and instruction on preparing fancy foods for their own parties and/or small catering business. These requests originated with homemakers, individual hostesses, cake decorators, caterers and many others wanting to be artistic with foods.

There have been previous books on catering, but those were designed primarily with the "professional" in mind--people who made a full-time career catering and who were volume feeding large receptions, banquets, special parties and weddings.

The genesis of this book was a small manual for a "Creative Foods Seminar". But over the years, so much additional information and so many recipes and designs were added that it forced writing of a much more detailed publication (which you are <u>now</u> reading!).

The author, Esther Murphy, the chief designer for Mrs. Mayo's School, is an internationally known authority and teacher of Cake Decorating. She has designed this book for those with little or no knowledge of decorating but who possess a "creative soul" and a fondness for beautiful food.

The book is an extremely valuable tool for the busy person who has neither the time nor, perhaps, the inclination to seek out the information from the hundreds of sources it has taken the author years to compile.

The recipes and ideas were painstakingly formulated and collected and culled from personal experience, pamphlets, correspondence, magazines, trade journals, books, unsolicited letters, and, as Esther puts it, from "just plain ol' trading back and forth with friends, relatives and business associates...."

Throughout her career (which includes three published books on cake decorating), Esther has always maintained that decorating food was one of the most creative, yet least expensive "hobbies" or "pastimes".

The illustrations and decorating ideas are exclusively Esther's. And she has thoughtfully arranged the book in a logical, step-by-step outline to save the reader countless hours of valuable time.

Truly, then, this book <u>is</u>.

"A Complete Guide

to Fancy Food Decorating

<u>Anyone</u> Can Do...."

BOOKS BY ESTHER MURPHY

Mrs. Mayo's "Book of Creative Foods"

Mrs. Mayo's "How to Make a Wedding Cake"

"The Art of Creative Cake Decorating"

"Holiday and Party Cakes"

AUTHOR'S PREFACE

While my book is intended primarily for the creative person wishing to prepare fancy party foods, it can easily be adapted by anyone interested in catering on a limited basis. Supplying fancy foods for parties actually is part of the larger catering business.

This type of catering--sometimes called Party Foods or Party Tray Catering--is the kind of business you can start with almost no investment. Most of the equipment needed is lying in your kitchen. And catering goes hand-in-glove with the Wedding Cake/Reception business, in which thousands of people are now involved as both a challenging way to give vent to their creative nature and as a method to earn extra income. And today's economy being what it is, who among us couldn't use extra money?

If you're interested in catering as a business, you must read "<u>How to Make Money in Cake Decorating: Owning & Operating a Successful Business in Your Home</u>". Despite its title, most of the information is applicable to a home catering business because it discusses promotion, advertising, how to get customers and deal with customer problems, how to save money on taxes, how to deal with banks and the IRS, and a myriad of other useful & valuable topics.

(Check your local library for a copy, or see back of this book for more information.)

PLEASE NOTE:

I suggest reading the opening paragraphs and the general instructions in <u>each</u> chapter from which you want to prepare a recipe. Information in these opening sections will apply to some, if not all, of the recipes..BUT they will not be repeated as you come to that particular recipe later in the book. So, read first, <u>carefully</u>.

The equipment needed in preparing many of these foods, such as pastry bags, couplers, decorating tubes, miniature aspic cutters, spatulas, colors, etc. are normally available at local cake & food decorating supply stores. They are generally listed in the Yellow Pages under "Baker's Supplies" or "Cake Decorating Supplies".

In several instances, I've mentioned some "brand" names. This isn't meant to promote any particular company. It's just that I've found those items will produce better results than a similar brand.

Happy Partying!

Esther Murphy

I

═══VEGETABLE ARTISTRY═══

For a most unusual centerpiece, use fresh vegetables to make beautiful flowers in a bouquet you can eat! This floral piece can be made up a week ahead then wrapped in plastic and kept in the refrigerator.

MATERIALS & EQUIPMENT NEEDED

1 sm. Cauliflower
1 bunch Parsley
3 lg. round Radishes
3 sm. white Onions
  (boiling onions)
5 med. Turnips
1 Carrot

Round Toothpicks
Sharp Paring Knife
Sm. sharp Scissors
#10 Decorating Tube
Sm. Flower Cutters*
Liquid Food Coloring:
    Rose Pink
    Lemon Yellow
    Grape
    Royal Blue
    Moss Green
5"-6" wide mouth glass or
  deep plastic containers
Container for Bouquet**

*Flower cutters from 1" Aspic Cutter Set, or Violet & sm. Daisy Cutters from the Wilton Flower Garden Set (Gum Paste Equipment).

**Any shallow container (under 5" diameter) in which the cauliflower will set firmly is suitable. A round plastic dish or woven basket is fine.

PREPARATIONS FOR MAKING BOUQUET:

    Flowers & stems should be prepared 1-3 days ahead. For a bouquet 7 to 8 inches across, you will need 3 each of the turnip roses, onion mums & radish bachelor buttons, plus approx. 30 small flowers made with the flower cutters (see above). Instructions for making flowers, stems and complete bouquet follows.

STEMS: Soak round toothpicks in water colored to a <u>very</u> dark shade of moss green, using concentrated food coloring. (Not the diluted type from grocery store.) Test after an hour to see if dark enough. If not, leave in colored water until they're as dark as a real flower stem. Remove from water, roll between paper towels to get rid of excess water, then spread out on towel until completely dry.

SMALL FLAT FLOWERS: Peel turnip, then cut at least twelve 1/16" thin slices. Use violet cutter, or small aspic cutter, to cut 20 flowers from slices. Place in single layers between damp paper towels on flat surface (8" square pan, round pie tin, etc.).

Cut very thin slices, crosswise, from a carrot. Punch 30 centers from these with a #10 decorating tube. Place separately between damp towels on top of cutout flowers. (10 of these centers are for the flowers below.)

Enclose pan in plastic bag & tie, or wrap airtight in plastic. Store in refrigerator until time to use.

DAISIES: Use same method as for small flat flowers, except turnip slices are to be 1/8" thick and 10 daisies are to be cut. Mix grape coloring into a small container of water and drop daisies into it. Let soak for several minutes, or until flowers are a light shade of lavender. (Time depends upon how much coloring is in water.)

Store like the above flowers (single layers between damp towels, wrapped in plastic, then placed in refrigerator).

BACHELOR BUTTONS: Make these with radishes, as explained under "Relish Trays" in this chapter. For these flowers, however, peel the radishes first, then soak in water colored with Royal Blue. (Careful with the Royal Blue. It's very strong, doesn't take very much to color the water!) Cover container and place in refrigerator.

PLEASE NOTE: The containers for any flowers that are stored in water in the refrigerator, (like bachelor buttons, chrysanthemums and roses) should be wide mouth jars or deep, wide plastic bowls. Flowers usually spread out to twice their original size and would be impossible to remove from container after soaking. This also applies to the carved vegetables under "Relish Trays".

CHRYSANTHEMUMS: Peel small onion so it is approximately 1" in diameter.

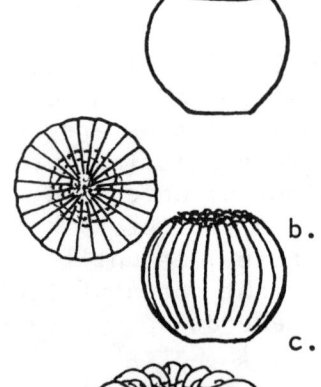

a. Cut top off so it is flat and none of the layers of onion are stuck together in the center. Cut bottom off just enough to make it smooth and all layers still firmly stuck together in the center.

b. Use very sharp paring knife to cut slices down from the top center to about 1/4" from bottom.

c. Soak in Lemon Yellow colored water in refrigerator. (See note above re: containers for soaking flowers in refrigerator.)

Sketch shows mum <u>after</u> soaking.

ROSES: Peel a turnip (no larger than 1 1/2" in diam.) as smoothly as possible. (If turnip is too large, cut it down to size.) Cut off top so it is flat.

a. Cut 5 slices around the outside, leaving attached at the bottom.

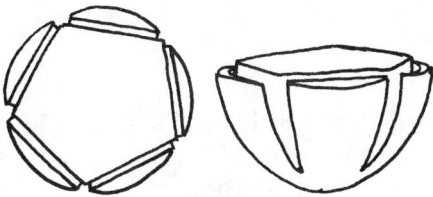

b. Cut off corners around center (shown as dark areas), almost down to base of petals. Pull these pieces out. (Use blunt tweezers for this.)

c. Cut a thin slice off the inside of each petal, slanting the knife outward, so the petal edge will be thin. Then, slice off the corners of center so it is round.

d. Repeat the same procedure as in "a" through "c" to make a second & third circle of petals, or, until the center is about 1/2" in diameter.

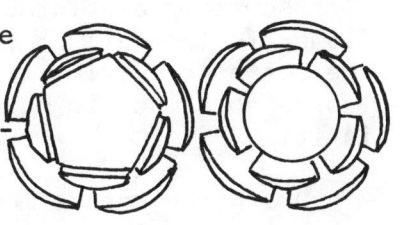

e. Mark 3 equal spaces around center. Start at a marking and cut a slice approx. one-third around in direction shown by arrow. Cut two more slices, then cut thin like the outer petals.

15

f. Cut center into a rounded cone shape with blunt point on top, then cut three curved grooves down the side.

g. Use small scissors and cut corners off petals to make round shapes.

Soak roses in pink colored water in refrigerator.

PLEASE NOTE: Be sure to place flowers in large top containers as mentioned previously under Bachelor Buttons.

MAKING THE BOUQUET

Cut the bottom of the cauliflower to the shape of the container, flat, round, or whatever. Be sure all the stems are intact on bottom. If the cauliflower is too tall or too large around the sides for the container, trim it off. It should fit snugly inside so as not to move around when placing flowers in it.

Drain the roses, mums and bachelor buttons on paper towels, then stick a green toothpick in bottom of each flower. These larger flowers are to be placed evenly over the cauliflower, i.e. stick a rose in one side, leave a space, then a mum - space - a bachelor button, then repeat. Be sure the picks are pushed firmly into the white portions of the cauliflower, not in between or in the sides of any stems. Also, the picks should not be pushed down too far. There should be at least 1 1/4" of pick showing. (See opposite page.)

Rest of the bouquet is filled in with the smaller flowers. Stick toothpicks in between large flowers all over the bouquet, then sprigs of parsley pushed down in between toothpicks & flowers. Push small flowers & daisies onto points of toothpicks, then centers.

   Place parsley into edge of container so some will hang over sides. If there are empty spaces where cauliflower is visible, fill in with parsley.

   This bouquet will keep fresh for a week in the refrigerator if covered with plastic wrap.

NOTE: If the bouquet is to be kept in refrigerator for any length of time, don't add parsley 'til ready to use.

Relish Trays

When an occasion calls for a relish tray----buffet, cocktail party, sit down luncheon or dinner, picnic----almost any combination of the foods listed below will make an attractive and appetizing dish.

Raw Vegetables	In Jars or Cans
Radishes	Ripe Olives, pitted
Green Onions	Green Olives, stuffed
Celery	Cherry Peppers
Cauliflower	Gherkins
Carrots	Dill Pickle Slices
Broccoli	Cocktail Onions
Cherry Tomatoes	Whole button Mushrooms

The raw vegetables can be simply washed & trimmed or some of them cut into decorative shapes (as per following instructions). In either case, they should be soaked in water and placed in refrigerator several hours or overnight. (Drain on paper towels before serving.)

RADISHES:

Buy bunches of radishes that still have the stems and tails intact (not the packages with everything trimmed off). Wash thoroughly. Do not scrape any portion of the red skin off unless absolutely necessary to remove dirt or black spots.

Cut green stems off, <u>leaving about 1/2" on</u> radish. Cut root ends off as described for each design.

(See opposite page for details on making radish roses, fans & bachelor buttons.)

Roses

Cut root end off so white circle is about 1/2" in diam. (depending upon radish size). Cut 5 slices around the outside, leaving bottom of slices attached to stem.

REMEMBER: When cutting into radishes for any of these designs, do not cut completely through to the bottom. The petals must stay attached.

Fans

Cut root end off so white circle is as small as possible. Cut a row of slices across radish as shown.

Bachelor Buttons

Cut root end off so white circle is large (about one-third way down radish). Cut slices across one way, then the other to make bunch of petals.

NOTE: Be sure to place these radishes in container with large top. They will all spread out when soaked in cold water.

ONION TASSELS:

Cut green stems off short. Cut roots off. Cut onions into thin slices, making sure they're all attached to stems.

CARROT CURLS:

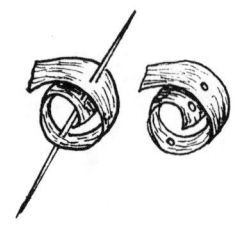

Use potato peeler to cut thin slices (lengthwise) off scraped carrot.

Roll into curl & fasten with toothpick. Soak in cold water, drain & remove pick. Curl will hold shape.

CAULIFLOWERETS:

Cut small sprays with stems, keeping as much the same size as possible.

BROCCOLI SPRAYS:

Use same method as for Cauliflowerets.

CELERY FANS:

Cut wide stalks in half, use narrow stalks as is. Cut both to about 3 inch lengths. Cut one end into slices for relish tray.

To use Celery stalks as stirrers for glass of vegetable juice or bloody Mary:

Cut stalks to at least four inches in length (depending upon size of glasses to be used). Don't slice these stalks into fans. Use small stalks near center (with leaves), if they're at least three inches long.

□ □ □ □ □

II

APPETIZERS

Included in this chapter are perhaps the most popular appetizers served at cocktail parties or before a meal: canapes, hors d'oeuvres and dips. Some are favorite old time classics, others you will find are new, different, easy-to-prepare and provide not only savory food for guests, but great conversation pieces as well.

Canapes

Canapes are like miniature open faced sandwiches. They're made from an endless variety of fillings placed on top of crackers or small pieces of toast and are usually decorated.

Most cookbooks and many women's magazines have recipes for making canapes, many of which have to be prepared at the last minute, so the crackers or toast will still be crisp when served.

Described on this, and the following pages, are new and practical ideas for making canapes. They can be prepared ahead of time and frozen to serve as a surprise for unexpected guests, or for a planned party to avoid a last minute rush to get the work done.

The secret is to freeze fillings that have been made and decorated on wax paper. Before serving time, they are taken out of the freezer and placed on a variety of crackers or toast. Thawing time: less than 30 minutes. The fillings stay fresh and the toast and crackers stay crisp!

Making Canapes to Freeze

Fillings that include cream cheese in the mixture, or any type of cheese spread that softens to a paste consistency, are the best for making canapes to freeze, since the mixture is soft enough to spread or squeeze through a decorating tube and become firm enough in the freezer for easy removal from the wax paper. Liverwurst, deviled ham and any finely ground meat, such as ham or chicken, also can be used when mixed with a little cream cheese or mayonnaise.

Seasoned Cream Cheese (described later in this chapter), used as a base with a variety of toppings (such as are listed under "Garnishes") are the quickest and easiest canape fillings to make for freezing. The use of pastry bags & couplings with decorating tubes will make the work go faster and the fillings more attractive. You do not have to be a cake decorator to squeeze fillings out of pastry bags!
NOTE: Information on using pastry bags & couplings with decorating tubes is at the end of chapter on "Desserts". Also, there is a variety of "squeeze" cheeses available in grocery stores. They are excellent for this purpose.

Fillings to be frozen should be made in the general shape of the crackers or toast you plan to use. There are many different shapes and sizes of crackers, so the type you choose determines the shape and size of the fillings. Also, the fillings should be made at least 1/4" smaller all around than the crackers.

After preparing the fillings (recipes on following pages), place them in separate pastry bags with couplings and attach the desired decorating tube. The enlarged sketches of designs for canapes follow recipes and designate the tube to be used as well as the movement made with the tube to obtain the design. (NOTE: Several fillings in the sketches are simply spread on with a small spatula.)

Before you make the fillings, plan on what type of containers you will use for freezing. For example, you may have on hand such things as flat candy boxes, shoe box tops, or even pie tins. Any container that is small enough to be wrapped in plastic or tied in a plastic bag, and flat enough to be stacked, is suitable. The wax paper on which you make the fillings must be cut to the shape of the container and slightly smaller in size.

There are several ways to make the fillings, the simplest of which is to (a) trace around the crackers on a piece of paper, place wax paper over the tracings, then (b) make fillings to fit within the tracings and decorate and (c) place wax paper with fillings into container to be wrapped and frozen.

NOTE: For any design that includes parsley, leave parsley off for freezing. Place on filling <u>after</u> removing from freezer.

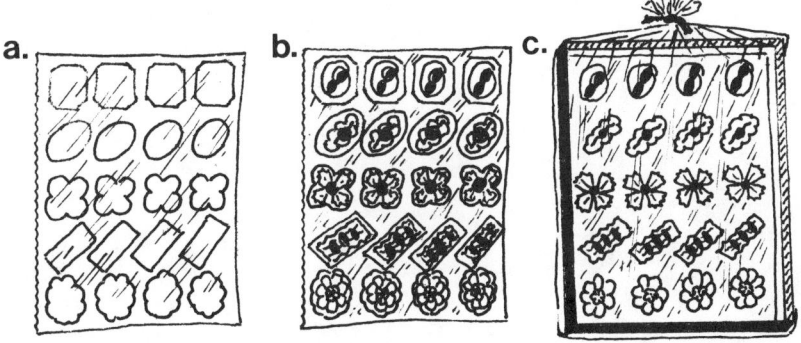

If you wish to make fillings on wax paper without tracing around crackers, you can sort of estimate the shape, but just be sure the fillings are all smaller than the actual crackers. Or....the crackers themselves can be placed under the wax paper and fillings made over them.

Freezing Canape Fillings

   Place wax paper(s) with fillings into container(s), wrap or tie in plastic bag(s). Each piece of wax paper should have its own container and <u>not</u> be stacked on top of one another inside the same container. They may be stacked <u>after</u> being wrapped or tied in bag.

Serving the Canapes

   Remove containers from freezer. Place wax paper with fillings on counter. Lift fillings off paper with end of small spatula and place on appropriately shaped cracker. Place on serving tray. Canapes can be served approximately 25 minutes later.

FILLINGS FOR CANAPES

NOTE: For any filling that includes chopped food in the recipe, food must be chopped extra fine. Many of the designs are made by squeezing filling through a decorating tube, and large lumps will clog the tube.

Also, each filling must have a solid base that will freeze. For example, if stars/shells made with a #32 tube are squeezed around edge of design, then one also must be squeezed in the center to make the solid base. If filling is spread on with small spatula, be sure there are no empty spaces.

Seasoned Cream Cheese

1 pkg. (8 oz.) Philadelphia Cream Cheese, softened
1 tbsp. mayonnaise

Place cream cheese in mixer and whip until fluffy.

Add mayonnaise, salt & pepper to taste and/or any other desired seasonings, such as paprika, onion salt, celery salt, etc.

Blend well, then place in pastry bag with coupling.

       Makes 35 to 40 fillings.

Deviled Ham Spread

4 1/2 oz. can deviled ham
4 oz. (1/2 of 8 oz. pkg.) soft Phila. Cream Cheese
2 teas. finely chopped gherkins

Place cream cheese in mixer and whip until fluffy. Add ham and gherkins and blend.

         Makes 30 fillings.

25

Jalopeno Pepper Cheese Spread

1 cup (8 oz.) finely shredded sharp natural cheddar cheese.
4 oz. (1/2 of 8 oz. pkg.) soft Phila. Cream Cheese.
2 teas. pickled jalopeno pepper, drained & finely chopped.
1 teas. pimiento, chopped fine.
1 teas. green pepper, "   "
Salt to taste
Dash of cayenne pepper

Whip cream cheese in mixer until fluffy. Add rest of ingredients, blend, then whip until smooth.

           Makes 25 fillings.

NOTE: Jalopeno cheese mix may be purchased already prepared. It can be squeezed through decorating tubes after being softened at room temperature and mashed up until smooth.

Anchovy Spread

2 tbsp. anchovy paste (discard liquid that comes out of tube).
3 oz. pkg. Phila. Cream Cheese, softened.

Blend together. This mix can be used for base of canape filling, or for decoration squeezed out on top of a Seasoned Cream Cheese filling. (Top it with a sprig of parsley <u>after</u> removing from freezer.)

Tasty Toppings

Place 1/2 teas. of any of the following on top of a seasoned cream cheese filling:

 Mix 2 teas. mayonnaise with 1/2 cup flaked & boned salmon,

   or....
   1/2 cup drained & flaked tuna

   or....
   1/2 cup finely chopped shrimp

Delicious Fillings from Left-Overs

1 cup (packed) of any of the following, finely chopped in blender or sliced thin, then snipped into fine pieces with scissors:

    Chicken--turkey--ham--beef--pork

1 teas. sour or dill pickle, finely chopped
1 teas. onion, finely chopped
3 tbsp. cream cheese, softened
1 tbsp. mayonnaise
Salt & pepper to taste

Blend all ingredients until smooth. If too lumpy to squeeze through decorating tubes, spread on wax paper with small spatula.

    Each mixture makes approx. 30 fillings.

Great Garnishes

Anchovy strips, pressed between paper towels to remove liquid.
Anchovy paste
Asparagus tips
Capers, drained
Chives, chopped
Cocktail onions, halved or whole
Cucumber slices
Egg Yolks and/or whites, boiled & sieved
Gherkins, sliced
Green onions, chopped
Mushrooms, sliced sideways
Olives, stuffed green, sliced
Olives, black, sliced or quartered
Pimientos, strips, chopped or cut into designs with small aspic cutters
Paprika
Parsley
Sesame seed, toasted
Radishes, sliced thin

DESIGNS FOR CANAPES

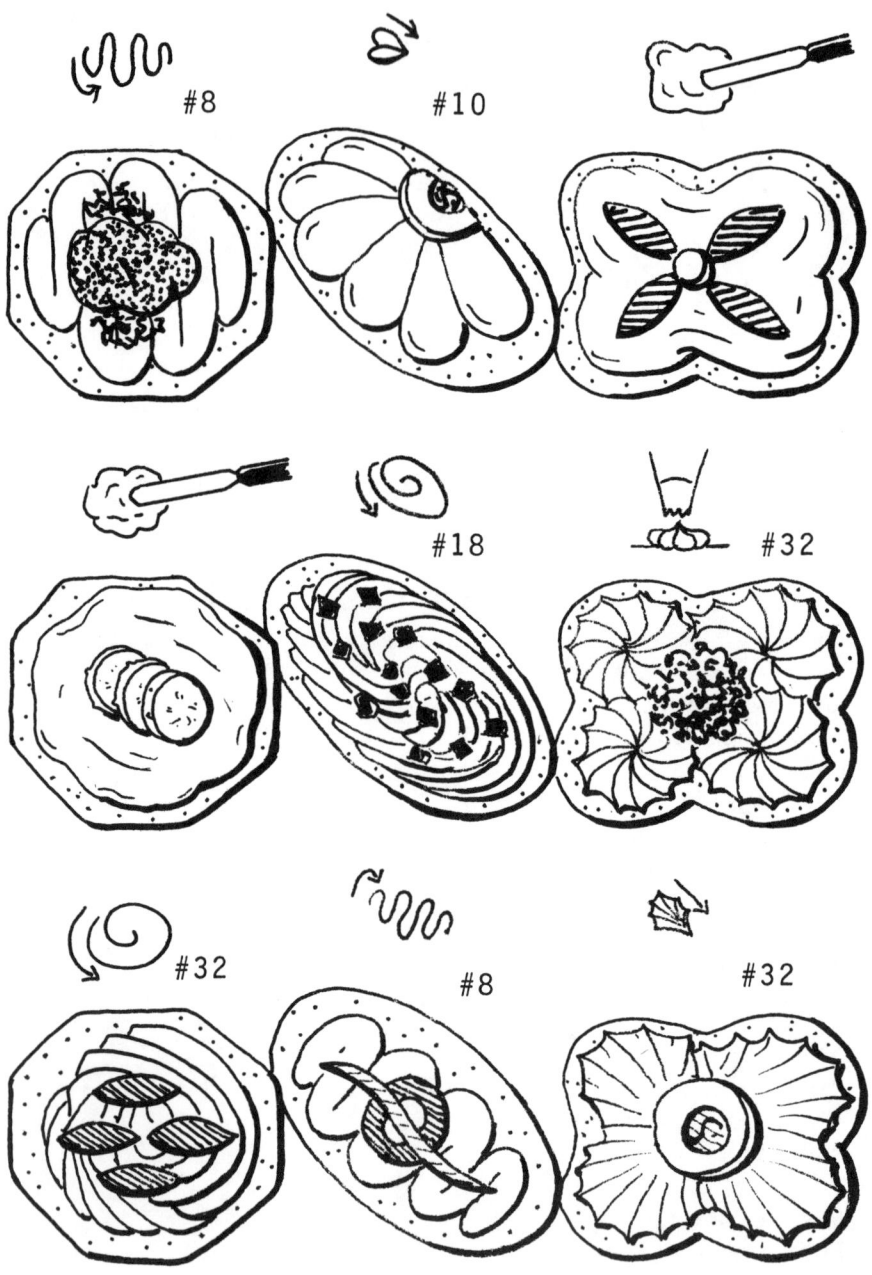

DESIGNS FOR CANAPES

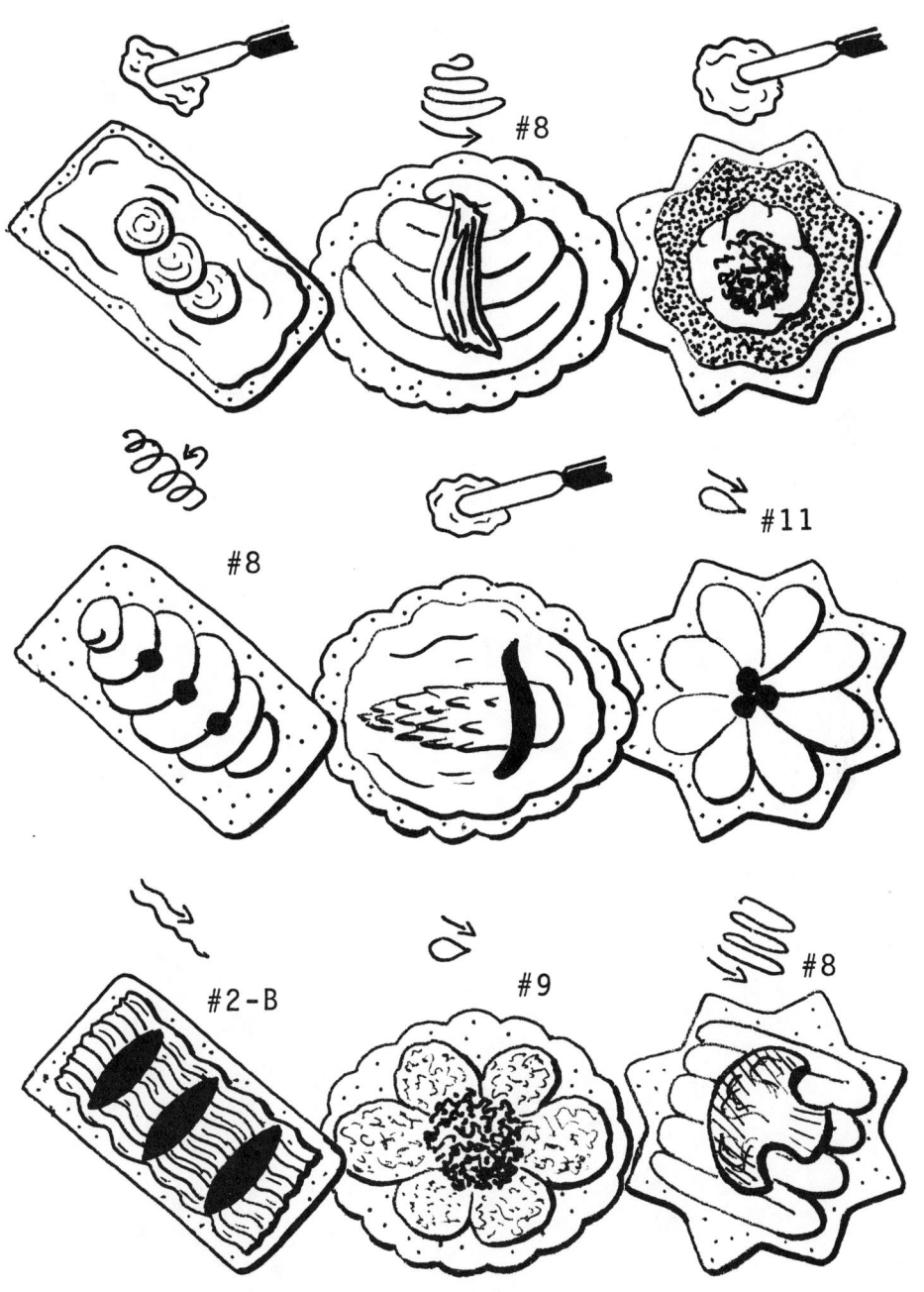

Hors d'Oeuvres

Hors d'oeuvres are usually served, either as appetizers, to stimulate the appetite before a meal, or, as the only food at a cocktail party. The word is French, pronounced "or derv" (like "serve"), and means "outside of work".

An hors d'oeuvre can be anything from a piece of cheese on a toothpick to a mushroom stuffed with a savory sausage filling. There is no end to the variety that can be made. Whether hot or cold, this is one food where you can let your imagination run absolutely wild!

Hot Hors d'Oeuvres

Hot hors d'oeuvres means just that...hot! Serve them from warming trays or chafing dishes on a buffet table, or from small trays passed among the guests at a cocktail party. The trays should not be overloaded. The hot hors d'oeuvres may be cold by the time half of them are eaten!

SPICY COCKTAIL MEATBALLS

3/4 lb. ground beef
4 oz. liver spread (Braunschweiger)
1 teas. prepared mustard
1/2 teas. salt
1/8 teas. pepper
1/4 cup fine dry bread crumbs
1 egg, slightly beaten
2 cups corn flakes, crushed (3/4 cup)

Combine ground beef, liver spread, mustard and seasonings 'til well blended. Add crumbs and egg, then mix thoroughly. Shape into 1-inch balls, using a rounded teaspoon of meat mixture for each. Cover tightly and refrigerate overnight.

Just before baking, roll in crushed corn flakes. Bake on rack in shallow pan in 350°F. oven for 10 min. Turn once and bake 10 min. more. If desired, garnish platter with a fan of tomato wedges.

Makes about 60 meatballs.

TUNA BALLS

1 - 12 1/2 or 13 oz. can tuna, drained
3/4 cup dry bread crumbs
2 eggs
1/2 cup minced onion
1 teas. salt
Dash pepper
Hot-Mustard Sauce (recipe next page)

Early in day or the day before serving:

Grease a cookie sheet or 9" x 13" baking pan. In a large bowl, with mixer at medium speed, mix well, all ingredients except sauce, occasionally scraping bowl with rubber spatula. Shape mixture into about 50 small balls, place on cookie sheet, then cover and refrigerate.

About 30 min. before serving:

Preheat oven to 450°F. Uncover and bake tuna balls 15 min. or until hot. Stick toothpick in each and serve with dish of Hot-Mustard Sauce.

Makes about 50 Tuna Balls.

Hot-Mustard Sauce

In a 2-quart sauce-pan, combine 1/4 cup dry mustard, 1/4 cup cider vinegar, 2 tbsp. sugar, 1/8 teas. salt and 1 egg. Over low heat, cook until mixture is just thickened, stirring constantly. Refrigerate mixture until cool. Stir in 1/2 cup mayonnaise. Serve cold with tuna balls.

BARBECUED PORK RIBLETS

1 1/2 lbs. pork ribs (Have the butcher cut the rack of ribs in half, or thirds, depending upon their original length....should end up with ribs about two inches long, and cut into single rib portions.)

Barbecue Sauce

1 med. size onion, sliced thin
2 tbsp. vinegar
3 tbsp. Worcestershire Sauce
1 1/2 teas. dry mustard
1/2 cup chopped celery
2 tbsp. brown sugar
1 cup water
2 tbsp. butter or margarine
4 tbsp. lemon juice
1 cup catsup

Brown onion in butter in small skillet.
Add other ingredients for sauce and cook over med. heat.
Brown ribs in small amount of oil in large skillet while sauce is cooking.
Pour sauce over browned ribs in skillet, cover, then let steam until ribs are tender (about 45 minutes).

CRESCENT FRANKS

1 pkg. (8 oz.) frozen Crescent rolls
16 cocktail franks
Small can sauerkraut
Mustard

Cut each roll triangle in half. Spread each with prepared mustard and drained sauerkraut.

Roll up the 16 franks in dough triangles. Bake at 375°F for 15 minutes. Serve hot.

OLIVE-FILLED CHEESE BALLS

1 cup (1/4 lb.) shredded sharp Cheddar cheese
2 tbsp. butter
1/2 cup flour
Dash cayenne
25 medium olives, stuffed green or pitted black

Cream together cheese & butter. Blend in flour and cayenne. Wrap a teaspoonful of dough around each olive, covering completely. Bake in a hot oven 400°F.) for 15 minutes. Serve on toothpicks.

                              Makes about 25 balls.

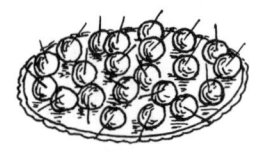

SAUSAGE STUFFED MUSHROOMS

1 1/2 lbs. fresh mushrooms (med. size, about 30)
1 1/2 lbs. ground pork sausage
1/2 cup shredded Mozzarella cheese
1/4 cup seasoned bread crumbs

Gently pull stems from mushrooms. Chop stems & set aside, separately from mushrooms.

Cook sausage until well browned in 10" skillet over medium heat, stirring often to keep separated. Use slotted spoon to remove sausage to drain on paper towels. Spoon off all but 2 tbsp. drippings from skillet.

Cook mushroom stems in hot drippings over medium heat until tender (about 10 minutes), stirring frequently. Remove skillet from heat, stir in sausage, cheese & crumbs.

Preheat oven to 450°F. Fill mushroom caps with sausage mixture.* Place stuffed mushrooms on cookie sheet and bake about 15 minutes.

*Mushrooms can be stuffed the day before, covered with plastic wrap, then placed in refrigerator overnight and baked next day just before serving time.

Makes 30.

HOT KABOBS

(Also, see Cold Kabobs under Cold Hors d'Oeuvres)

HAWAIIAN KABOBS

1 lb. ham, cut into 20 3/4" cubes
20 chunks pineapple
2 tbsp. brown sugar
2 tbsp. vinegar
4 tbsp. soy sauce

Two ways to make these tasty kabobs:

Spear cubes of meat & pineapple on toothpick.
Broil in electric broiler, turning frequently and
    brushing with mixture of sugar, soy sauce &
    vinegar until hot & slightly browned.

OR.....

Saute' meat & pineapple in lightly buttered skillet.
    Brush with mixture of sugar, soy sauce & vinegar
    and stir frequently. When hot & slightly browned,
    spear cubes of meat & pineapple on toothpicks.

NOTE: Either of the above may be prepared & cooked
    beforehand, then reheated in slow (300°F.)
    oven until hot.

VARIETY HOT KABOBS

For an almost endless variety of Hot Kabobs, alternate
2 or 3 of the following:

    Cocktail onions   Cubed cooked chicken
    Cherry Tomatoes   Small shrimp
    Whole mushrooms   3/4" pcs. frankfurter
    Cubed boiled potatoes   Cubed bologna
    Cubed cooked beef   Miniature cooked meatballs
        Cooked sausage balls

Broil on toothpicks or spear after saute'ing.

Cold Hors d'Oeuvres

COLD KABOBS

Cold Kabobs are an Americanized version of the original "kabab" (Persia - Hindustan) or "kebap" (Arabia - Turkey), defined as "cubes of meat (as lamb) marinated & cooked with onions, tomatoes, or other vegetables, usually on a skewer". The American word is pronounced exactly the way it's spelled, "ka-bob", with accent on the first syllable.

Change the above ingredients to food that's already cooked and chilled, use wooden skewers or cocktail picks and you have "cold Kabobs".

They can be prepared beforehand, placed in refrigerator on trays (covered with plastic wrap), ready for serving.

Spear 2 or 3 (or more) of the following on the skewers or toothpicks:

Cubes of ham
Chunks of pineapple
Mandarin orange slices
Cheese cubes
Melon balls

Chicken cubes
Canned cocktail sausages, cut in half
Cubes or slices of pickle
Stuffed green olives
Pitted black olives
Whole mushrooms, canned or fresh
Cherry tomatoes
Cocktail onions

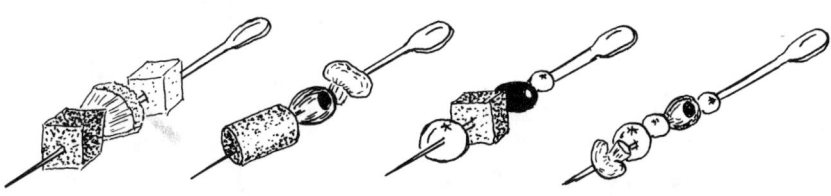

(Also see Kabobs under "Hot Hors d'Oeuvres")

DEVILED EGGS

Deviled Eggs may be considered a common dish to be served at picnics, luncheons, buffets, etc. But they also can be made into elegant appetizers to serve at parties as hors d'oeuvres. Make them up as far as 2-3 days in advance, place in an airtight container and keep in refrigerator.

RELISH DEVILED EGGS

12 eggs, boiled & peeled
 2 tbsp. (slightly heaped) sweet pickle relish, drained thoroughly.
 2 tbsp. mayonnaise
1/4 teas. dry mustard
Salt to taste

Makes 20 deviled eggs.

(See General Instructions starting below)

OLIVE & PICKLE DEVILED EGGS

12 eggs, boiled & peeled
Chop fine:
    2 teas. black olives
    1 teas. green onions
    2 teas. stuffed green olives
    1 teas. dill pickle
2 tbsp. mayonnaise
1/2 teas. lemon juice
1/4 teas. dry mustard
Salt & pepper to taste

Makes 20 deviled eggs.

GENERAL INSTRUCTIONS FOR MAKING DEVILED EGGS:

Put 12 eggs into 4 qt. pot and cover with cold water. Add 1/4 cup vinegar to water (makes eggs easier to peel). Bring to a boil, then reduce heat. Stir eggs about every 2 minutes so the yolks will be in the center of the hard boiled eggs. Cook about 10 minutes. Plunge eggs in cold water for 5 minutes. Crack all shells while in cold water. Remove shells.

Set under cold running water to cool completely. Cut in half lengthwise and remove yolks. Use a small, sharp paring knife and slice a small portion of the undersides of the egg whites. (This will keep eggs setting upright before and after filling.)

Press all yolks + 4 egg whites + white scraps through sieve. Mix thoroughly with ingredients in either of preceding recipes.

Set egg whites in rows on wax paper and use a 12" pastry bag with coupling and a #22 decorating tube. Fill this with the egg mixture.

Squeeze just enough egg mixture into each egg white so it is level with the rim of the white. Go back over the eggs and squeeze a mound of the mixture on each by starting almost at the outer rim and going 'round and 'round with the tube until you reach the center.

DECORATING DEVILED EGGS:

Use any or all of these materials & designs......

Quartered bl. olive. Pimiento center.

Quartered bl. olive. Pimiento strip.

Pimiento strips.

Stuffed gr. olive slices.

Parsley. Pimiento strips.

Whole pimiento cut w/sm. aspic cutters.

Anchovy strips. Paprika.

Sliced bl. olive. Pimiento strip.

Anchovy strips. Parsley.

Dips

DILL VEGETABLE DIP

1 cup mayonnaise
1 cup sour cream
2 teas. dill weed
2 teas. parsley flakes
2 teas. finely chopped green onion
1 teas. Lawry's seasoned salt

Mix all ingredients together and let set for at least 1 hour before serving.

Good for dipping vegetables, such as celery, cauliflower, broccoli, cucumber, cherry tomatoes, green peppers, etc. Also good as a dip for corn chips & small wheat crackers.

Keeps for at least 2 weeks in airtight container in refrigerator.
Makes 2 cups

SPINACH DIP

2 cups mayonnaise
1/2 cup chopped fresh parsley (cut with scissors)
1/2 small onion, finely chopped
1 small clove garlic, minced
1 tbsp. lemon juice
1/4 teas. pepper
1 10 ounce pkg. frozen, chopped spinach, thawed & drained on paper towels.

Blend all ingredients in covered blender at high speed just until finely chopped. Cover, refrigerate at least 4 hours.

Makes 2 3/4 cups

This dip is great with potato and corn chips.
(Can be made one or two days before serving.)

GREEN ONION DIP

1 cup sour cream
1 envelope beef flavored bouillon
1/4 cup finely chopped green onion
1 teas. Worcestershire sauce

Mix all ingredients, cover & place in refrigerator for at least 1 hour before serving.

Serve with potato or corn chips.   Makes 1 cup

OLIVE PIMIENTO CREAM CHEESE DIP

1 8-ounce pkg. cream cheese, softened then whipped.
1/3 cup mayonnaise
3 tbsp. finely chopped stuffed green olives
Dash of white pepper

Mix all ingredients together. Can be served immediately, or covered & placed in refrigerator overnight. If latter, let set at room temperature for at least 2 hours before serving.

                                                        Makes 1 1/2 cups

Great with any kind of small cracker or green vegetables.

TUNA DIP

1 6-ounce can tuna, washed, drained & chopped very fine.
1/2 cup mayonnaise
2 teas. lemon juice
2 tbsp. finely chopped green onion
1 teas.   "   "   dill pickle

Blend all ingredients together. Chill at least 1 hour before serving.

                                                    Makes 1 1/3 cups

Serve with Melba toast or Rye-Crisp.

SHRIMP REMOULADE

Remoulade is a classic sauce sometimes used for shrimp cocktails, but can also be used as a dip for shrimp. The French word is pronounced "Rim-oo-lod", with accent on the first syllable, and "oo" like in "spoon" and "lod" like in "cod".

Remoulade Sauce has a mayonnaise base, rather than the traditional catsup base used for shrimp cocktails.

Shrimp are available frozen, cooked & deveined, fresh, frozen in the shell, or canned. Easiest to use are the frozen, cooked & deveined. They may be found in very small or medium sizes. Takes about 60 very small shrimp to make a pound, but only 25-30 medium ones. If using very small shrimp for dips, stick at least two or three on a toothpick, but only one per toothpick for medium ones.

For 6 shrimp cocktails, use 1 lb. medium size shrimp and the following recipe for sauce. For dips, double the sauce recipe for 1 lb. of shrimp, either size.

Recipe for Remoulade Sauce

1 cup mayonnaise
2 teas. prepared mustard
2 tbsp. chopped gherkins
2 tbsp. capers
1 teas. minced onion
1 teas. anchovy paste
1/2 teas. paprika
4 teas. chili sauce
    1/2 teas. each, salt & pepper

Blend all ingredients together. For shrimp cocktail, arrange shrimp on lettuce and top with sauce. For shrimp dip, serve in bowl on tray with shrimp on toothpicks arranged around bowl.

III

PARTY SNACKS
IN DECORATIVE SHAPES

A party snack tray need not be just an array of cheese and lunch meat slices...it can be a beautiful display of decorative shapes molded from various mixtures of cheeses and meats. Sliced and served on crackers, they make delicious snacks and add a festive touch to the refreshment table.

Such shapes as logs and balls may also be wrapped as gifts for various occasions. Or, using the same recipes, the mixtures can be rolled into small balls and served on toothpicks as hors d'oeuvres.

Here are some choice recipes for making these unusual party snacks:

CHEDDAR CHEESE LOG

2 pkgs. (8 oz. ea.) cream cheese, softened
2 cups (8 oz.) shredded sharp natural cheddar cheese
1 tbsp. chopped pimiento
1 tbsp. finely chopped onion
1 tbsp. chopped green pepper
2 teas. Worcestershire sauce
1 teas. lemon juice
　Dash of cayenne pepper
　Dash of salt

3/4 cup finely chopped pecans

Combine cream cheese and cheddar cheese, mixing until well blended. Add rest of ingredients except pecans. Mix well. Chill 1 hour.

(Recipe continues on next page)

Roll mixture in wax paper to form two logs, each about 5" long and 1 1/2" in diameter. Chill for 1 hour.

Unwrap, roll in nuts and re-wrap in clean wax paper. Chill for several hours.

Yield: 40 - 1/4" slices of log or 40 - 3/4" balls.

VARIATIONS:

Shape into large ball. Coat all over with chopped parsley or pecans.

Shape into small balls. Roll in chopped nuts, finely chopped dried beef, toasted sesame seeds, or chopped parsley, etc.

DEVILED HAM ROLLS

4 cans (4 1/2 oz. ea.) deviled ham
3/4 cup stuffed green olives, finely chopped
4 pkgs. (3 oz. ea.) cream cheese, softened
4 teas. prepared mustard

Mix ham and olives. Chill until firm. Divide into 4 pieces, then form into 4 rolls, about 1 1/2" in diameter. (See "Cheddar Cheese Log" for "how to".) Wrap in wax paper and chill again.

Whip cream cheese in mixer until fluffy. Add mustard and blend. Unwrap rolls and place on wax paper on shallow tray or pan. Spread cream cheese mixture over rolls like frosting. Cover lightly with wax paper and chill for several hours.

Decorate with sliced stuffed green olives & parsley or strips of pimiento & black olive slivers.

Yield: About 36 1/4" slices.

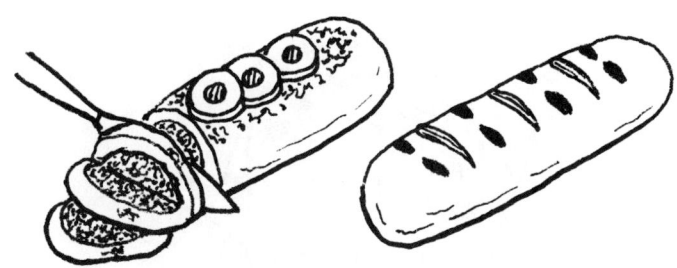

BLUE CHEESE PARTY BALL

3/4 cup crumbled blue cheese (about 4 oz.)
1 pkg. (8 oz.) cream cheese, softened
1 cup shredded cheddar cheese (about 4 oz.)
1/4 cup minced onion
1 tbsp. Worcestershire sauce
Finely chopped parsley if making small balls.
Pimiento and black olives if making large ball.

Blend all cheese together until creamy. Blend in onion and Worcestershire sauce, then beat mixture at medium speed until fluffy. Cover and chill for several hours.

Shape mixture into 1 large ball or 40 small balls. Roll the small balls in chopped parsley and stick toothpick into each for serving.

To decorate the large ball, cut diamond shapes out of whole pimiento and round slices of black olives. Place these on the ball as shown below or use your own imagination. Whole black olives stuck on toothpicks can be placed all around the base of the ball.

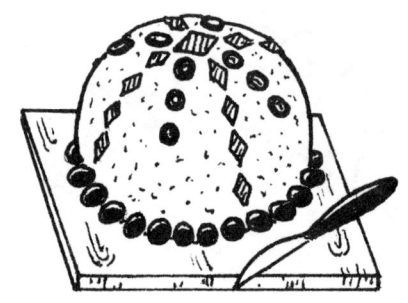

BRAUNSCHWEIGER PINEAPPLE

1 lb. Braunschweiger (2 - 8 oz. pkgs.)
2 tbsp. minced onion
2 tbsp. dill or sour pickle, chopped very fine
2 boiled eggs, sieved (press through wire sieve with
   rubber spatula or fingertips)
2 tbsp. mayonnaise

For decoration: stuffed green olives and green pepper.

Mix all ingredients (except decorations) together until well blended. Chill until firm. Slice about 20 stuffed green olives into thin slices while mixture is chilling. Mold with wet hands into shape of pineapple (like an egg setting upright on large end). Form hole in top about the size of a quarter. Chill again until very firm.

Remove from refrigerator. Using an orange stick (or smooth end of a crochet or knitting needle) dipped in water, score the mold as shown below with diagonal lines about 5/8" apart. Place an olive slice in each diamond shape made by the scored lines. Press very firmly on each slice so they stick. Chill again, then glaze (see recipe next page).

Glaze for Braunschweiger Pineapple

Stir 1 tbsp. (1 envelope) Knox Gelatine in 1 tbsp. cold water until softened. Dissolve 1 beef bouillon cube in 1 cup boiling water (or use 1 cup boiling Campbell's beef consomme). Chill until slightly thick, about the consistency of heavy cream. Set firmly chilled mold on rack with tray underneath & spoon glaze all over sides. Chill again, then re-glaze for best results. Hold in refrigerator until serving time.

To make pineapple top: Cut a large green pepper into sections, then cut pointed spears, ranging from about two inches to three, or as long as you can get out of the sections. Takes about 15 spears.

Stick these into the hole on top of pineapple <u>after</u> it has been glazed.

To serve: Set on plate in ring of parsley surrounded by crackers.

Yield: About 40 servings.

SALMON PARTY SQUARES

1 - 16 oz. can (2 cups) salmon
1 - 8 oz. pkg. cream cheese, softened
1 tbsp. lemon juice
2 teas. grated onion
1 teas. prepared horseradish
1/4 teas. salt
1 teas. liquid smoke

For coating and decorating:
    1/2 cup chopped pecans
    4 tbsp. snipped parsley (use scissors)
    Whole pimiento to make fish design

Drain and flake salmon, removing skin and bones. Combine salmon with next 6 ingredients. Mix thoroughly. Chill several hours.

Shape mixture into two 1 1/2" diameter square loaves. (Do this by first making a roll, then pressing into square shape with wide spatula to make smooth sides and square corners.) Chill.

Combine pecans and parsley, spread out on wax paper. Press mold down into mixture on all four sides.

Cut several fish from thinly sliced pimiento and place on top of mold. Use thinly sliced black olive and a #5 decorating tube to make eyes for fish.

Yield: About 40 servings.

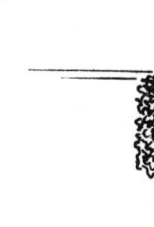
Pattern

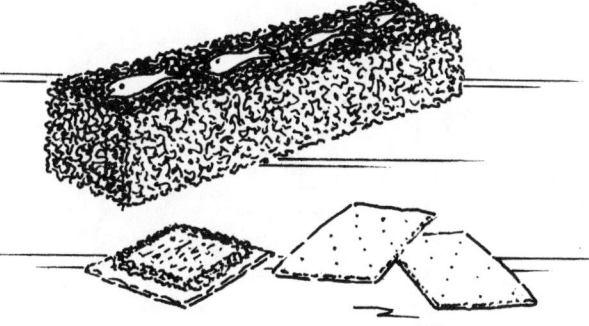

IV

══TEA SANDWICHES══

The word everybody uses to describe tea sandwiches is "dainty". And what other word could there be? They are small, they are thin, their flavorings are subtle and delicate; they are often fashioned into fragile rolls, pinwheels, ribbons, checkerboards, rounds; and they are always arranged on serving platters with infinite care and attention to appearance.

A variety of breads (preferably thin sliced) should be used for tea sandwiches. White and whole wheat breads are the most versatile, equally delicious with almost all sandwich fillings. Rye bread should be used only with strong-flavored fillings, such as sausage, deviled ham and sharp cheese.

Bread for sandwiches should be 2-3 days old because it is easier to slice and cut. It is also easier to cut if chilled first. The crusts should <u>always</u> be removed.

When making large quantities of sandwiches, prepare the fillings first. Figure on 1 tbsp. of filling for each tea sandwich. Make one kind of sandwich at a time, and complete the entire process before starting another. Don't try to make too many kinds or too many shapes. Pick three or four basic shapes among pinwheels, checkerboards, ribbons, roll-ups, etc.... add a few open face sandwiches to each serving tray for color appeal and garnish trays with such things as parsley sprigs, sliced stuffed olives, pimiento strips, sliced black olives, etc. Be sure to have enough sandwich trays to allow for a perfect display...that is, with no piling or overlapping to diminish the beauty of the show.

Tea sandwiches may be made the day before the party and refrigerated, or made several days in advance and frozen. In either event, they must be in airtight containers or wrapped completely in plastic wrap.

Closed, flat or rolled sandwiches, such as ribbons, checkerboards and pinwheels, should be wrapped separately, <u>uncut</u>. They can then be stacked in layers and stored. Open faced sandwiches must be placed in a single layer on tray to store.

For sandwiches that are to be stored, spread each bread slice with softened butter or margarine. DON'T spread with mayonnaise, salad dressing or jelly as these soak into the bread. (Mayonnaise, however, may be used in the filling mixtures.)*

Sandwiches will thaw in 1-2 hours. Open-face thaw most quickly. Don't remove outer wrapping until sandwiches are partially thawed. Time the thawing so sandwiches are ready just in time for serving. If not served immediately, hold in refrigerator.

*Gelatine Mayonnaise: (Used in very moist fillings)
    Mix 1 teas. Knox unflavored gelatine with 2 tbsp. cold water until softened. Stir over boiling water until dissolved. Add this warm gelatine mixture to 1 cup mayonnaise and blend thoroughly.

FILLINGS FOR TEA SANDWICHES

HAM & OLIVE SPREAD:

    2/3 cup minced cooked ham
    1/2 cup minced stuffed olives
      2 tbsp. minced parsley (snip with scissors)
      1 tbsp. Worcestershire sauce
    1/4 cup mayonnaise

Blend together until smooth.   Makes 24

EGG RELISH SPREAD:

      4 hard-boiled eggs, seived
      2 tbsp. drained sweet pickle relish
    1/8 teas. dry mustard
      Salt & pepper to taste
      2 tbsp. mayonnaise

Blend together until smooth.   Makes 20

CHICKEN SALAD SPREAD:

Mix together:
      1 cup minced cooked chicken or turkey
    1/2 cup minced celery
      2 teas. minced onion
      1 teas. minced sour pickle
Salt & pepper to taste
      2 tbsp. mayonnaise   Makes 24

DEVILED HAM-HORSERADISH:

Blend together:
    1 can (3 oz.) deviled ham
    1 pkg. (3 oz.) cream cheese
    1 tbsp. horseradish
    2 tbsp. mayonnaise   Makes 20

LIVERWURST:

    Blend together until smooth:
      8 oz. liverwurst
      1 teas. minced onion
      1 hard-boiled egg, sieved
      1 teas. mayonnaise
      Dash of Worcestershire sauce
      Dash paprika   Makes 20

PICKLED ONION CRAB:

    Mix together:
      1 cup flaked crabmeat
      3 tbsp. mayonnaise
      1 tbsp. chopped cocktail onion
      Dash of salt & paprika   Makes 20

SEASONED BUTTERS FOR TEA SANDWICHES

All tea sandwiches don't have to have fillings of meats, chicken, fish, etc.. Butter, combined with various seasonings, make real tasty sandwiches, when used on the bread alone.

PIMIENTO BUTTER:

    1/2 cup (1 cube) butter or margarine, softened
    4 tbsp. sieved pimiento
    2 tbsp. mayonnaise
    Few drops Tabasco sauce

    Blend together thoroughly.

This butter makes delicious tea sandwiches. Spread slice of thin whole wheat bread with pimiento butter; cover with slice of white bread. Spread this with Green Pepper Butter*, then top with another thin slice of wheat bread. Press together. Wrap in plastic wrap. Chill for at least 1 hour or longer, or, if made several days beforehand, freeze.

* GREEN PEPPER BUTTER:

    1/2 cup butter or margarine, softened
    4 tbsp. finely chopped green pepper

    Blend together until smooth

1 recipe each of these two mixes will make 4 stacks of bread.

To serve: Trim all crusts off. Cut crosswise twice, making three strips from each stack. Cut across center of strips, making six sandwiches from each of the four stacks of bread.

HERB BUTTER:

    1/2 lb. softened butter
    1 teas. parsley flakes
    1/2 teas. sweet basil
    1 teas. chive flakes
    1/2 teas. thyme

    Blend together thoroughly.

    May be used as is to spread on tea sandwiches or chilled just enough to form into an attractive shape, such as a rosette for an individual serving, made with a large, #4, star pastry tube (not cake decorating tube). Squeeze rosettes out on wax paper, then chill 'til firm enough to remove from paper and still keep shape.

    To use on Herb Bread, melt the butter first, mix in the herbs and brush over French bread slices with pastry brush. Then, toast in oven.

MISCELLANEOUS "BUTTERS" --- Savory and sweet.

Any of these butters can be used on tea sandwiches, such as ribbons, mosaics, pinwheels, checkerboards, etc.

Blend butter or margarine with seasonings below until creamy:

- Anchovy paste, lemon juice & chives
- Chives, parsley or mint, snipped, with lemon juice.
- Honey and a bit of lemon juice.
- Horseradish or mustard: Well-drained bottled horseradish or prepared or dry mustard.
- Lemon or orange: Grated rind and juice, plus nutmeg.

RIBBON SANDWICHES

Alternately stack 3 slices whole wheat & 2 slices white bread, spreading each slice with any of the recipes for "Fillings".

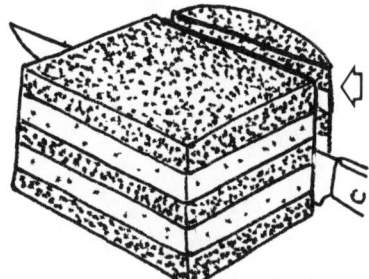

Firmly press together each stack of slices. Then, with a sharp knife, using a sawing motion, slice crusts from all sides of each stack.

Arrange stacks in shallow pan (cookie sheet). Cover with wax paper and slightly damp cloth. Chill for at least several hours. Then cut into 1/2" slices.

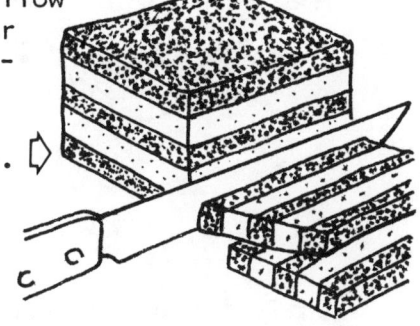

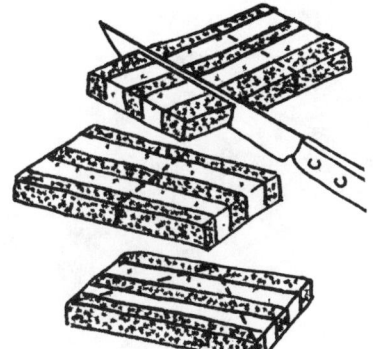

After cutting the 1/2" slices, cut each slice into thirds, halves, or 2 or 3 triangles, as shown.

CHECKERBOARDS

For each stack, alternate 2 slices of whole wheat and 2 slices of white bread, filling as in Steps 1 and 2 of Ribbon sandwiches.

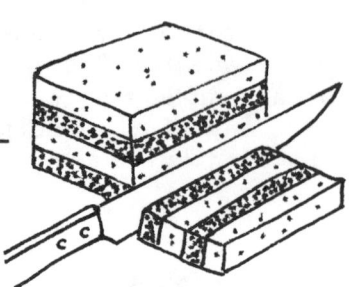

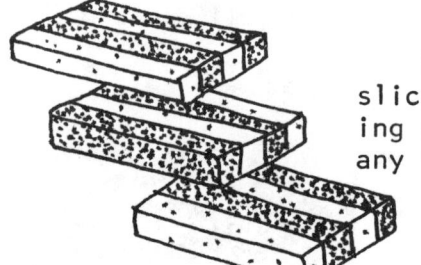

Cut each stack into 1/2" slices. Then put 3 alternating slices together, using any filling or spread.

Chill for at least several hours. Remove from refrigerator. With sharp knife, immediately make checkerboard slices, 1/2" thick.

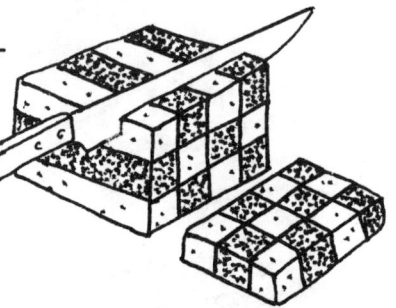

MOSAICS

Inlaid designs made with dark & light bread.

Make two at a time! Cut 2 dark & 2 light bread rounds. Remove center of 1 light & 1 dark round with small, round cutter, as below. Then insert small round of dark bread into hole of large light ring, and small round of light into large dark ring.

Spread solid round with butter or margarine, then filling. Cover light round with dark mosaic and dark round with light mosaic. Only imagination limits the variety of mosaics you can make.

Use one-half inch aspic cutters to form small hearts, diamonds, etc. that fit into larger sizes of same shapes. Alternate centers (light and dark) on top layers of sandwiches as above rounds. Or cut rounds of light & dark bread into wedges and alternate on top of solid round of bread.

   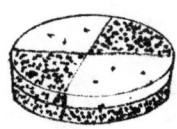

LILIES

Trim crusts from fresh white bread slices. Cut one corner off. Spread thickly with filling. Roll as shown, two corners overlapping. Use a carrot strip or trim a piece of cheddar cheese to a round, pointed shape to make center of lily. Place this into center of roll. Put a toothpick through lily to hold while chilling in refrigerator. Remove pick before serving.

ROLL-UPS

Trim crusts from fresh bread slices. Press out with rolling pin. Spread completely with seasoned butter. Lay any of the following across the end of each slice: Vienna sausages, asparagus tips, sweet pickles. Roll up.

Serve whole, or cut in halves or thirds, with a bit of water cress or parsley tucked in one or both ends. If made ahead, place in refrigerator, seam side down, until time to serve.

ENVELOPES

Cut crusts from thin slices of <u>fresh</u> rye or whole wheat. Spread with filling completely. Fold as shown, placing toothpick through bread, then refrigerate. Remove pick to serve.

PINWHEELS

Trim crusts off slices of fresh whole wheat and white bread. Place three alternating slices side by side. Run rolling pin over each slice. (Makes bread easy to handle, less likely to crack.)

Spread softened butter or margarine on top and in between each slice, then filling across top. Place 3 or 4 stuffed green olives, 2 gherkins, a frank or 2 vienna sausages across one end. (If using olives, place them lengthwise across the bread slice so they will be sliced sideways when the sandwich is cut.)

Starting at end with stuffed olives (or whatever), tightly roll bread up, as you would a jelly roll, being careful to keep sides in line. Tight rolls will make for easier slicing.

Wrap rolls individually in plastic wrap, fastening ends securely. Chill for several hours or overnight. (Or make ahead, wrap, freeze, then let thaw about 45 minutes before slicing.)

Cut chilled rolls into 1/4 to 1/2 inch slices. Lift with broad spatula onto serving plate. Or, place on tray in layers with wax paper between and on top, then a moist cloth. Chill for later use.

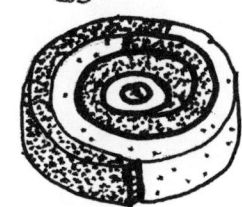

V

GELATINE SALADS & ASPICS

Most gelatine dishes, whether they're salads, main dishes or desserts, are made by using the same basic rules. Please read the following before preparing any recipe in this chapter:

- Gelatine should always be stirred in cold water first, then, either brought to a boiling point over heat, or, boiling water poured over it.

- If making layers of different gelatines in the same dish, make sure each layer is completely jelled before adding another layer.

- If you use canned fruits and wish to add juice to gelatine, be sure to deduct same amount of water as amount of juice being added.

- Use only canned pineapple in gelatine, not fresh.

- Chill clear gelatine until slightly jelled before adding any ingredients, then mix together. Makes everything more evenly distributed.

- When pouring balance of gelatine (whether clear or containing other ingredients) over design in bottom of mold, be sure design is chilled and completely jelled.

- When placing mold in refrigerator, it must set exactly level on shelf.

UNMOLDING GELATINE DISHES

a. Dip mold into warm water (not hot) to depth of gelatine.

b. Loosen around edge with the tip of paring knife.

c. Place serving dish on top of mold and turn upside down. Shake slightly, holding serving dish tightly to mold. If gelatine does not unmold readily, repeat.

After gelatine is unmolded, chill again to make sure surface is completely jelled.

MAKING A DESIGN IN THE MOLD

Mix 1 envelope Knox unflavored gelatine in 2 tbsp. cold water until soft. Add this to 1 1/4 cups boiling water and stir until dissolved. Chill until consistency resembles unbeaten egg white. Place mold you plan to use in refrigerator to chill.

Remove mold and spoon in just enough gelatine to cover bottom. (If mold has indented designs in bottom, put gelatine into these only. The design you make can be incorporated with the indentations.) Chill until jelled.

Depending upon the design you plan, slice or cut into decorative shapes, vegetables, meats or fruits. Press any of these into gelatine in bottom of mold in planned design, then chill again until completely jelled.

Pour a thin layer of gelatine over design and chill again until jelled.

Now the entire gelatine mixture (containing whatever ingredients called for in recipe) can be poured into mold over the design. Chill in refrigerator for at least 3 to 4 hours before unmolding. (Time depends upon depth of mold.)

NOTE: The remaining clear gelatine used in making the design will keep for a month or more in a jar in refrigerator. It can be remelted over low heat when needed again.

COTTAGE CHEESE SALAD
(Serves 12)

1 envelope Knox unflavored gelatine
1 tbsp. granulated sugar
1/2 teas. salt
1/2 cup water
2 cups (16 oz.) cottage cheese
2 tbsp. horseradish
1/2 cup heavy cream, whipped
2 cups diced apple (2 med. apples)
1/2 cup finely diced green pepper

For decorating: Pimiento, green onion tops & black olives.

a. Mix gelatine, sugar and salt thoroughly in small saucepan.

b. Add water. Place over heat and stir until barely comes to boil. Remove from heat and keep stirring until gelatine is completely dissolved.

c. Sieve or beat cottage cheese on high speed in electric mixer. Blend in gelatine mixture.

d. Fold in remaining ingredients. Place in refrigerator until cool, but not jelled.

MAKING THE DESIGN (Instructions next page)......

The mold is made in an 8" spring form ring pan with a design on bottom of pan. An ordinary ring pan or round cake pan also may be used to make the same design.

Spoon clear gelatine into indentations in mold as described in "Making a Design in the Mold", or, cover bottom with gelatine if pan is flat.

Cut 18 flowers out of whole pimientos with small aspic cutter, or Briar Rose cutter from Wilton's Flower Garden Set (Gum paste cutters). Cut a hole in the center of each flower with a #10 decorating tube. Cut black olives into four sections (from top to bottom), then slice to make thin. Cut flower centers out of slices with black <u>skin</u>, using the #10 tube. Cut green onion tops into <u>narrow</u> slivers, about 1 1/2" long to make the flower stems.

Press a flower and a center into the clear gelatine in each indentation. Press a stem on each side of the flowers. Chill until completely jelled, then pour chilled cottage cheese salad mixture over design and chill until firm, about three to four hours. Unmold and garnish around base with salad greens, such as watercress, parsley, etc.

MOLDED VEGETABLE SALAD
(12 servings)

2 envelopes Knox unflavored gelatine
1/2 cup granulated sugar
1/2 teas. salt
2 1/2 cups water, divided
1/2 cup lemon juice
24 thin slices unpeeled cucumber
1 1/2 cup thinly sliced radishes
1/2 cup finely shredded cabbage
1 cup diced celery

For decorating: 17 thin slices unpeeled cucumber
                 32 thin slices radishes

a. Mix gelatine, sugar and salt thoroughly in a saucepan.

b. Add 1 cup of the water. Stir over heat until just to boiling point. Remove from heat immediately.

c. Stir in remaining 1 1/2 cup water and lemon juice.

d. Make design in bottom of a 9" Wilton Petal Pan with decorating vegetables, using the method described previously in this chapter.

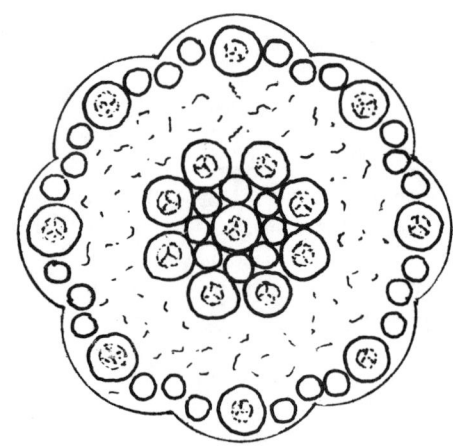

e. Chill the gelatine mixture (a, b & c) to un-
      beaten egg white consistency.

f. Fold in remaining vegetables. Pour into mold
      (over completely jelled design) and chill
      until firm.

g. Unmold on serving platter and garnish with salad
      greens.

Aspics

*Aspic: A savory jelly used cold to make a mold of
meat or vegetables. (Also, see "Garnish for
Serving Tray" near end of chapter on Chaud
Froid Buffet Molds for clear decorating Aspic.)*

BASIC BEEF OR CHICKEN ASPIC

(6 servings)

1 envelope Knox unflavored gelatine
2 cups water, divided
2 bouillon cubes, beef or chicken
1/4 teas. Worcestershire sauce
1 teas. grated onion
Dash of pepper
1 3/4 cup diced cooked meat and vegetables*

a. Stir gelatine in 1/2 cup of the water to soften.

b. Add bouillon cubes. Place over heat and stir
      until barely reaches boiling point.

c. Remove from heat and add remaining 1 1/2 cup water,
      Worcestershire sauce, onion and pepper.

(Continued next page)

IF YOU WISH TO MAKE A DESIGN IN BOTTOM OF PAN, NOW is the time to do it! (Suggestion: Small, thin slices of meat and/or vegetables, placed alternately around edge of mold.)

d. Chill gelatine mixture (a, b & c) to unbeaten egg white consistency.

e. Fold in meat and vegetables. Pour into a 4-cup mold or individual molds and chill until firm.

f. Unmold on serving plate and garnish with salad greens.

*Suggested combinations:

- 1 1/4 cups diced cooked chicken and 1/2 cup cooked, seasoned vegetables.
- 1 1/4 cup diced, cooked ham and 2 hard boiled eggs, chopped.
- 1 cup diced, leftover meat, 1/2 cup diced celery and 2 tbsp. chopped green pepper.

TOMATO ASPIC

(8 servings)

2 envelopes Knox unflavored gelatine
3 1/2 cups tomato juice, divided
1/2 teas. salt
1 teas. sugar
1 teas. Worcestershire sauce
1/4 teas. tabasco
4 tbsp. lemon juice

a. Stir gelatine in 1/2 cup tomato juice to soften.

b. Place over heat and stir constantly until barely comes to boiling point. Remove from heat & keep stirring until gelatine is dissolved.

c. Stir in remaining tomato juice & seasonings.

d. Pour into 4-cup mold or individual molds.

e. Chill until firm.

f. Unmold on serving plate.

g. Garnish with salad greens, cucumber slices and black olives. Serve with salad dressing.

VI

PARTY SANDWICH LOAVES

Sandwich Loaves can be served for many different occasions, including buffets, cocktail parties, teas or any type of party when you wish to serve your guests really good food! The loaves can also be decorated to serve as a centerpiece or even decorated like a birthday cake, complete with a greeting.

Any one of the following recipes will fill one layer of either of the two types of sandwich loaves described in this chapter. The recipes can be used in different combinations or, if preferred, one recipe can be used throughout the whole loaf.

FILLINGS FOR SANDWICH LOAVES

EGG SALAD

Combine 6 hard-boiled eggs, chopped fine, with the following:

> 1 teas. each (finely chopped) stuffed green olives, black olives, green onions and sweet pickles.
> 1/4 cup mayonnaise
> Salt & pepper to taste
>
> NOTE: A pastry blender makes a good utensil for chopping boiled eggs.

HAM SALAD

Mix 1 1/2 cups cooked ham (ground or snipped fine with kitchen shears) with the following:

    1/3 cup chopped, sour pickles
    1 teas. prepared mustard
    1/2 cup mayonnaise

CHICKEN SALAD

Combine 1 1/2 cups finely chopped boned chicken breasts with the following:

    3/4 cup finely chopped celery
    1 tbsp. minced onion
    2 tbsp. finely chopped green pepper
    1/2 cup mayonnaise
    Salt & pepper to taste

TUNA SALAD

Substitute drained & flaked tuna for chicken in above recipe.

SALMON SALAD

Mix 7 or 8 oz. can salmon, drained, boned & flaked with

    2 teas. minced onion
    1 teas. lemon juice
    1/4 cup chopped black olives
    1/4 cup mayonnaise
    Salt & pepper to taste

OLIVE NUT CREAM CHEESE SPREAD

1 8-oz. and 1 3-oz. pkg. cream cheese, softened
2 tbsp. mayonnaise
2 tbsp. chopped stuffed green olives
3 tbsp. chopped pecans
Salt & white pepper to taste

Whip softened cream cheese with electric mixer until fluffy. Blend in other ingredients by hand, using large spoon.

THE LONG, SQUARE SANDWICH LOAF

Trim crusts from 6 slices white and 6 slices dark bread. Lay 3 slices of either white or dark end to end on cardboard covered with wax paper. "Scrape" a very thin layer of butter or margarine over (and in between) slices. This sticks slices together and, when refrigerated, butter keeps fillings from soaking into bread. Spread any desired filling over slices.

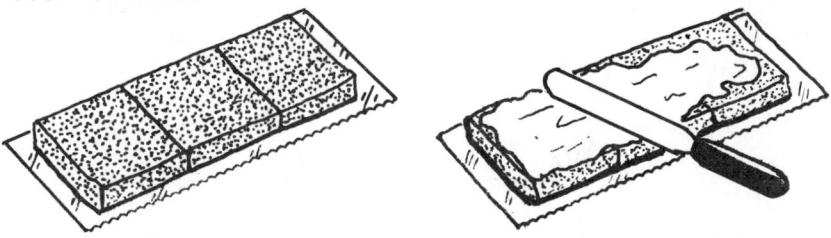

Butter both sides of the next two layers and one side of the top layer. Spread fillings over the second and third layers, then set top 3 slices of bread in place, buttered side down. Press down slightly but not enough to make the fillings ooze out.

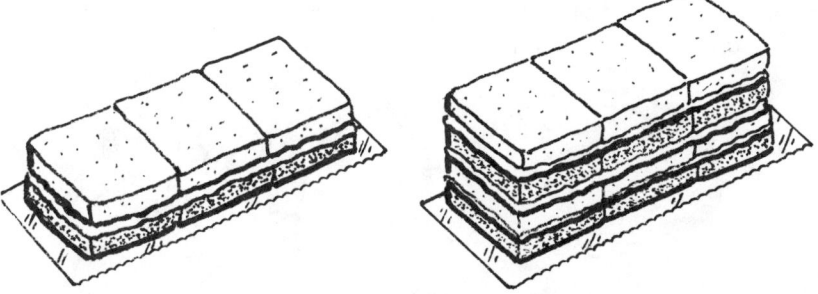

Wrap in plastic wrap and set in refrigerator for several hours or overnight. Remove from refrigerator & place on serving plate. "Crumb" the loaf by spreading a very thin layer of frosting cream cheese mixture (described on next page) over the whole loaf. Using the same mixture, frost the loaf with a thicker layer (like icing a cake). Return to refrigerator until time to decorate.

RECIPES FOR CREAM CHEESE FROSTING

FOR FROSTING SANDWICH LOAVES:

Use electric mixer to whip 3 8-oz. pkgs. softened cream cheese until fluffy. Add 1/2 cup mayonnaise, salt & white pepper to taste, then mix at medium speed until blended.

FOR DECORATING:

Use 1 tbsp. mayonnaise with 1 8-oz. pkg. cream cheese and mix by same method. Add salt & white pepper if desired.

THE OVAL SHAPED SANDWICH LOAF

Cut 4 slices from each center of a round loaf of light rye and a round loaf of pumpernickel bread. Butter slices (same as for long loaf) and place fillings in between, then wrap and place in refrigerator. Crumb and frost in the same manner, then decorate.

(Decorations for sandwich loaves are explained in detail on the following pages.)

DECORATING SANDWICH LOAVES

There are several ways of decorating sandwich loaves, two of which are described here. (1) The cream cheese for decorating (recipe preceding page) will make borders and flowers when used with pastry bags and tubes, the same kind used to decorate cakes.

(2) Fresh vegetables, cut into various shapes with miniature cutters, can be used to make flat flower designs on the cream cheese frosted loaf.

NOTE: Tools mentioned in the following instructions, such as miniature cutters, pastry bags, tubes, etc., as well as books with basic decorating techniques, are obtainable from most cake decorating supply stores.

CREAM CHEESE DECORATIONS

For this birthday sandwich loaf, use the decorating cream cheese (recipe preceding page) and check instructions for using pastry bags and tubes in "Desserts" chapter.

To decorate the base, use uncolored cream cheese mixture and a #32 star tube to make shell border.

For leaves, color a small amount of cream cheese (about the size of a lemon) to a medium green. Place in pastry bag with #67 leaf tube.

For the flowers, color two separate amounts of cream cheese (each about the size of a lemon) to a medium pink and lavender (or any two colors you wish). Place each in a separate bag, one with a #140 drop flower tube, the other with a #129 drop flower tube. For flower centers, color cream cheese (about the size of an apricot) to a medium yellow and place in bag with #3 round tube.

Squeeze a wreath of leaves around the top edge, then squeeze alternating colored flowers over the leaves. Squeeze a small dot in center of each flower.

To write or print a greeting on top, attach a #4 tube to bag with one of the flower colors. Scratch line(s) lightly across top with a toothpick to keep lettering straight. (It's better to see guidelines, than to get the lettering crooked!)

VEGETABLE DECORATIONS ON SANDWICH LOAF

Use miniature cutters (petit four, aspic or miniature cookie cutters), to form flower shapes.

Slice a turnip very thin, then form flowers from slices. To make different colored flowers, soak in separate cups of water, colored with liquid colors, for ten minutes or so, depending upon how dark the colored water is. Press on paper towels to remove excess moisture.

Make centers for flowers by cutting black olives in fourths, then slicing them to get a flat, thin piece of the skin. Cut little round pieces with a #10 decorating tube to place in centers. (See instructions for Flower Spray Design in chapter on "Chaud Froid Buffet Molds" for more details.)

Leaves are made from green pepper skins (sliced same as olives). Make leaf shapes with scissors. Long, curved stems are slivers of green onion stems, cut with sharp paring knife. Press all pieces between paper towels before placing on loaf.

Soften 1 envelope (1 tbsp.) Knox gelatine in 2 tbsp. cold water, then pour 1 cup boiling water over it and stir until dissolved. Set in refrigerator until cooled (but not jelled).

Before setting decorations in place, dip each piece into the gelatine mixture, then press on the surface of cream cheese frosting. May be necessary to use tweezers for some of the pieces. Stick the little black centers on flowers in the same manner.

Use uncolored cream cheese mixture to make a "bulb" border around top (#7 tube) and base (#12 tube). Or, very small sprigs of parsley can be placed around top and larger sprigs around base.

These sandwich loaves can be frozen for as long as a week before using if placed in an airtight container. (If using parsley for borders, place on loaf <u>after</u> removing from freezer.)

VEGETABLES & CREAM CHEESE DECORATIONS

This is truly a spectaculer decoration for sandwich loaves and it is <u>very</u> easy to make! The horn of plenty is made with cream cheese but the vegetables are real.

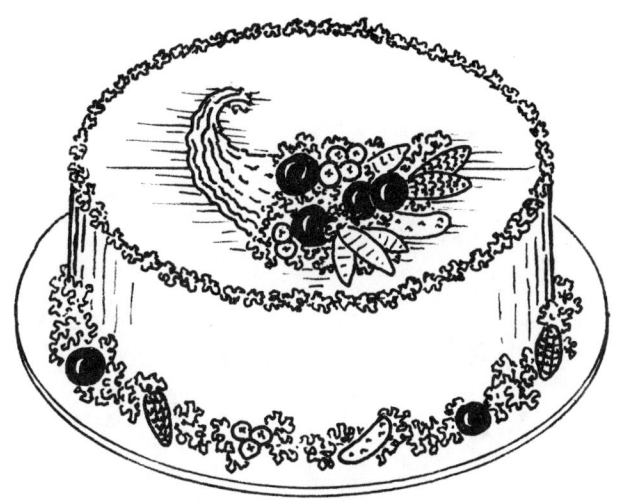

To make the horn, use an 8" pastry bag without a coupling and cut the end off to a slightly larger size, so when a #172 tube is placed down in it, the tip of the tube sticks out from the bag about 1/2". Color decorating cream cheese (about the size of a large orange) to a gold shade (Egg Yellow and Brown). Place in bag and twist top, then squeeze the horn out as shown on the following page.

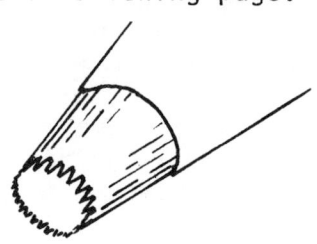

Begin squeezing on the bag with a rather light pressure, then increase it as you progress on the horn, moving the tube back and forth, as shown by the jagged line on the arrow. To make the large end of horn, the bag must be squeezed very hard so a large amount of cream cheese will emerge. Move the tube around in a circle at end.

NOTE: The horn of plenty can also be made by cutting off the large end of a curved, yellow squash at a slant.

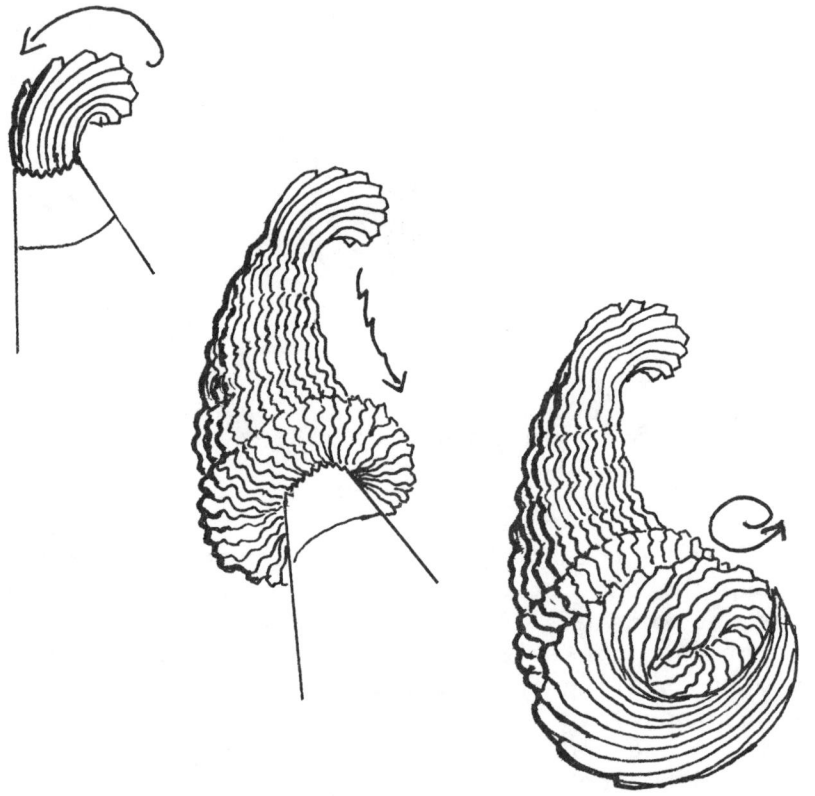

The vegetables coming out of the horn are miniature ears of corn (obtainable in small jars, usually in the gourmet section of the grocery), cherry tomatoes or sweet red cherry peppers, gherkin pickles (for cucumbers), cocktail onions and small carrots, carved with a paring knife from any regular size carrot.

Use the gelatine mixture under "Vegetable Decorations on Sandwich Loaf" (previously described in this chapter). Dip each vegetable in this before placing on horn and out on frosted loaf. Color a bit of cream cheese mixture with Leaf Green food coloring to stick vegetables together. Place sprigs of parsley in between and around vegetables, and chill until serving time. May be kept for several days in refrigerator if tightly covered. (In this case, however, the parsley should be set in place <u>after</u> the loaf is removed from refrigerator.)

The same vegetables can be placed around base of loaf at intervals with parsley in between. Push toothpicks into vegetables, then into side of loaf to keep in place.

◻ ◻ ◻ ◻ ◻

VII

CHAUD FROID
BUFFET MOLDS

These molds may serve as a centerpiece for a small buffet table or as one of a variety of dishes on a large buffet table. Chaud froid is a rich, creamed gelatine sauce that gives an even coating to the mold's surface. The sauce can be used to cover almost any prepared meat, fowl or fish and is usually decorated. Food to be covered with chaud froid is always chilled first, <u>then</u> covered.

(Chaud froid, pronounced "show frwa" is French and means "warm-cold". The sauce is first heated, then chilled for serving.)

RECIPE FOR CHAUD FROID SAUCE:

1/2 cup + 1 tbsp. water	1 teas. salt
4 tbsp. vegetable oil	1/8 teas. cayenne pepper
1/2 cup all-purpose flour	2 1/2 cups milk
2 envelopes Knox unflavored gelatine	1/2 cup light cream

Gently heat water & vegetable oil in 2-quart pan.
Mix in a bowl, the flour, gelatine, salt & pepper.
Remove oil & water from heat, add flour mixture & stir until smooth.
Slowly mix milk in & stir over heat until mixture comes to a boil.
Remove from heat, stir mixture over ice until slightly cool, then add cream.
Continue stirring until mixture barely coats the back of a stainless steel spoon.

This recipe is sufficient to cover any mold described in this chapter. Make the sauce <u>after</u> the mold is completed. (Recipes for molds near the end of the chapter.)

"How to use" chaud froid sauce with molds follows.

APPLYING CHAUD FROID SAUCE TO MOLDS

Before making mold, trace around the pan to be used on a corrugated cardboard. Cut out & set aside.

After mold has completely jelled, check directions for unmolding in chapter on Gelatine Salads & Aspics, and turn mold out on the cutout cardboard. Return to refrigerator until surface is firmly jelled. Make Chaud Froid sauce.

Place mold on rack over sheet pan. Pour sauce over it, letting drippings go down in pan. When completely covered, set back into refrigerator until sauce is firmly jelled. Scrape drippings from pan and return to chaud froid pan.

Set mold back on rack over pan and repeat above process. If, after being covered twice, surface of mold is still uneven, or not covered very good, repeat the process a third time. Refrigerate while preparing decorations.

DECORATING MOLDS COVERED WITH CHAUD FROID

Be sure to read this whole section before decorating any of the molds.

Decorations for these molds can be made with a variety of designs, using sliced, fresh vegetables, pimientos, black olives, stuffed green olives, etc. The decorations are made by cutting these items into various shapes, either with small paring knife, scissors, small aspic cutters and in some cases, even round cake decorating tubes!

Dipping Decorations

The decorations are dipped into chilled, clear gelatine before placing on the mold.

RECIPE: Dissolve 1 envelope Knox gelatine in 2 tbsp. cold water. Mix with 1 cup boiling water until dissolved. Chill, but don't let it jell.

Dip larger pieces of decorations into gelatine with fingertips. Smaller pieces, such as flower centers, lilies of the valley, etc. can be picked up with tweezers and dipped. Sounds a bit tedious, but is much more efficient than using your fingers to handle such small pieces.

Placing Decorations

Chaud froid covered molds must always be cold when placing the decorations. For example, when making a flower spray, take mold out of refrigerator, place stems on, then refrigerate a few minutes before putting flowers in place. Then chill again before putting on leaves.

Stems & Leaves

Stems are made from upper portions of green onions, leaves from green peppers. Parboil onion tops about six seconds in salt water. Remove and drop immediately into ice water to keep bright green color. Do the same with green pepper, except leave in boiling, salted water for about eight minutes, then drop in ice water. Press between paper towels to get rid of excess water before cutting into shapes. Cut narrow slivers from onion tops with paring knife for stems. Slice pepper skins off and cut leaves out of them with scissors.

Finishing Decorated Mold

After all decorations are in place on mold, add 1/2 cup cold water to gelatine used for dipping. (If the mixture has jelled slightly, place over low heat for a few minutes to melt.) Remove mold from refrigerator and use a large spoon to pour gelatine all over it. Store in refrigerator until serving time. If kept in covered container, molds will keep refrigerated for a week.

☐ ☐ ☐ ☐ ☐

FLOWER SPRAY DESIGN

This mold is made in an 8 1/2" x 2 1/2" deep spring form pan. Any size or shape pan may be used, as long as it holds one of the mold recipes (each of which are for a 6-cup pan).

Flowers in this design are made from radishes & carrots, with black olive centers.

Following the sketches, cut all pieces out before placing them on mold.

Cut black olive into 4 sections from top to bottom. Using a sharp paring knife, slice off the inside of two sections. Make three circles out of these sections with a #12 cake decorating tube for centers.

Slice centers of radishes paper-thin. They should be thin enough to be transparent. Make twelve slices, same size diameter as possible. Either throw the ends away or eat them!

For the daisy-like flower, make several long, very thin slices, lengthwise, from a carrot. Cut these into strips about 1/4" wide, then cut diagonally across the strips to make triangle shapes about 3/4" long.

Cut out stems & leaves (as previously described) and you are ready to decorate the mold. This sketch of the finished spray is smaller than the real one will be, but will help in knowing where to place the decorations. Set the stems on first, then the flowers and lastly, the leaves.

Cut thin slices of radishes in half and place around sides of mold, alternating the slices so one is up, the other down, etc. to make a wavy line all around the sides. Or, use half slices of radishes with circles of black olives (cut with #8 decorating tube) for a scalloped design around sides. Chill mold again.

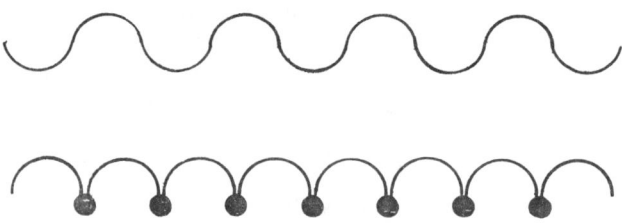

Cover whole decorated mold with gelatine as described previously, then garnish base as explained below.

GARNISH FOR SERVING TRAY

Jellied consomme and parsley make a perfect combination to decorate the base of the mold.

Use one 10 1/2 oz. can of Campbell's beef consomme and 1 envelope Knox gelatine. Soften gelatine in 2 tbsp. consomme first, then add rest of consomme and bring to a boil until gelatine is completely dissolved.

Pour this into an 8" square pan and chill until jelled. Unmold, chill again, then cut into squares about 3/8" across. Place these consomme cubes all around the mold, then set about four sprigs of parsley around the circle.

More Designs for Chaud Froid Molds

DAISY & LILY OF THE VALLEY SPRAY

    Here is a different type of flower spray you may wish to use. Daisy petals are cut from thin slices of turnips (soaked in pink colored water), using a small aspic cutter. Place these on mold first. Centers are cut from thin slices of black olives with a #8 decorating tube. Leaves & stems (as described previously) are placed on next, then lilies of the valley. Lilies are cut from thin slices of boiled egg white, using a #12 decorating tube to cut a circle, then a "bite" out of circle with the same tube.

GRAPE DESIGN FOR THE SUMMERTIME

or any other time!

This grape design can be used on a whole ham covered with chaud froid, a canned ham, or a ham mold made in a ham shaped can.

The grapes are made from red cabbage leaves (boiled separately about 10 minutes, then pressed between paper towels). Form circles with large end of any regular decorating tube - #5, #12, #16, etc. Leaves are cut from green pepper and stems & tendrils from green onion tops as described before.

A fitting decoration for the base of this dish is two or three colors of real grapes, red, black and green. They're also good eating with ham!

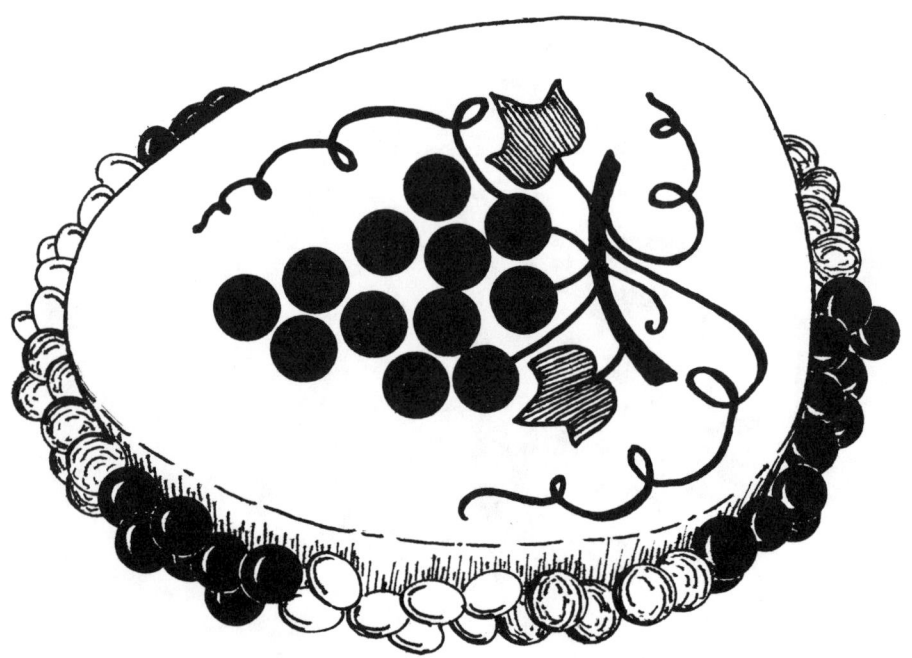

□ □ □ □ □

CHRISTMAS DESIGN

Make this chaud froid mold in a ring pan and decorate with a holly wreath.

Cut holly leaves with scissors from green peppers (boiled & sliced thin as previously mentioned), using pattern in sketch below.

Make berries and bow from pimientos (sliced thin), using #12 decorating tube for berries and a pair of scissors to cut bow from pattern.

Push parsley sprigs into chaud froid all around base of mold.

EASTER CHAUD FROID MOLD

Use one half of an egg shaped cake pan (8 3/4"x 5 3/4") to make a ham mold for this unusual Easter creation. (Recipe for mold at end of this chapter.)

Cover mold with chaud froid sauce, then decorate. The lines & dots are made by coloring 1 tbsp. chaud froid sauce blue, 2 tbsp. lavender and 3 tbsp. pink. Spread these colors out on wax paper to a thickness of 1/16". Chill, then cut 24 round dots from the blue sauce, using a #12 decorating tube. Cut 16 strips, 1" x 1/8" from the lavender, then 24 strips, same size, from the pink. Use recipe on Page 86 to make "dipping" gelatine. Lift the chaud froid cutouts from the wax paper with a small thin spatula, dip in the gelatine, then set in place on the chilled ham mold. Chill, then pour leftover gelatine over entire mold. Set back into refrigerator until serving time.

To make the chicks-in-eggs surrounding the mold, hard boil 12 eggs and peel. Cut whites in half (crosswise, not lengthwise) with a jagged line made with paring knife or, make your own cutter from metal strip on wax paper box. (Use long nosed pliars to bend strip where shown by dotted lines.)

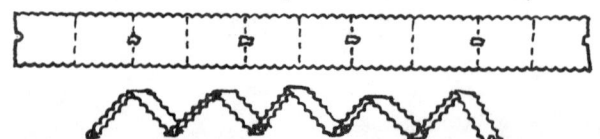

Gently lift large end of egg white off yolk and cut bottom off, so it will set upright. (The other half egg white & yolk will be used to make the chicken.) Repeat this with all 12 eggs, placing leftover whites & yolks in a bowl.

The half egg whites are to be colored pink, blue and lavender. To do this: Use three containers, each of which will hold four egg whites. Color (with liquid coloring) water in one bowl pink, one blue & one lavender. Soak the whites in bowls until they absorb enough color to make pastel shades. (Time soaking depends upon how much color is stirred into water.) Drain upsidedown on paper towels.

RECIPE FOR MAKING STUFFED EGG FILLING:

12 yolks & half egg whites (leftovers from preceding)
1/3 cup mayonnaise
1/4 teas. salt (slightly heaped)
1/8 teas. pepper
1/8 teas. dry mustard

Sieve the whites & yolks as follows: Chop slightly, then press firmly through fine strainer with back of spoon, or better still, your fingers. (Eggs have to be very fine to flow freely through coupling on pastry bag AND to make round shape for chicken head.)

Mix all ingredients together until smooth. Place into 8" pastry bag with coupling only (no coupling ring or decorating tube).

Squeeze filling into egg shell until it stacks up slightly above rim, then stop pressure on pastry bag. Start squeezing again (real hard) until a ball is formed on top. Stop pressure on bag and scrape end of coupling across top of ball, then lift off.

If point is left on ball, dampen finger and press down.

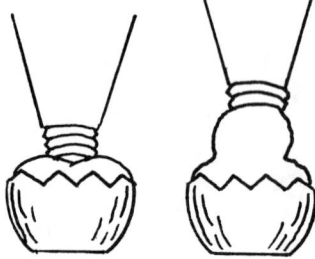

Cut eyes from sliced skins of black olives with #8 decorating tube and triangles (for beaks) from thin slices of carrot with paring knife. These are shown actual size in sketch.

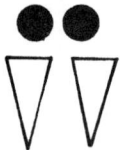

Stick eyes and beak on head. Eyes should stick to surface. Beak must be pushed into surface at angles, as shown in sketch of side view.

Place eggs around the mold at even intervals and sprigs of parsley around fronts of eggs.

NOTE: These chicks-in-eggs also make a terrific decoration for plain baked ham. Place around ham with parsley, as above.

Recipes for Chaud Froid Molds

HAM SALAD MOLD

3 cups finely chopped, cooked ham
4 tbsp. minced onion
1 cup mayonnaise
1 cup chili sauce
2 teas. horseradish
4 teas. prepared mustard
1/2 teas. Tabasco
2 envelopes (2 tbsp.) Knox unflavored gelatine
1 cup water

a. Grind ham, or chop it finely. Combine with onion, mayonnaise, chili sauce, horseradish, mustard & Tabasco.

b. Sprinkle gelatine on water to soften.

c. Place over medium heat and stir until comes to boil and gelatine dissolved.

d. Remove from heat and blend into meat mixture. Turn into 6-cup mold and chill until firm.

e. Unmold, chill, then cover with chaud froid sauce.

f. Decorate.

CHICKEN SALAD MOLD

2 cups (packed) finely chopped cooked chicken (cut with kitchen shears)
NOTE: 4 chicken breasts with ribs makes the correct amount.

Chop finely:
    1 1/2 cups celery
    2 tbsp. dill pickle
    3 tbsp. green onions
    1 tbsp. pimiento
    2 tbsp. black olives

1 cup mayonnaise
1/2 teas. salt
Dash of pepper

2 envelopes (2 tbsp.) Knox unflavored gelatine
1 cup water, divided

a. Mix all ingredients together except last two. Chill.

b. Soften gelatine in 3 tbsp. water. Boil rest of water and pour over softened gelatine. Stir until dissolved. Chill only (not jelled).

c. Mix chilled gelatine into meat mixture and pour into 6-cup mold, then chill until jelled.

d. Unmold. Cover with chaud froid sauce and decorate.

TUNA SALAD MOLD

2 envelopes (2 tbsp.) Knox unflavored gelatine
3 1/2 cups milk, divided
4 egg yolks
2 teas. salt
Dash pepper
2 teas. prepared mustard
2 cans (6 or 7 oz. ea.) tuna, drained & flaked fine
4 tbsp. lemon juice
1 cup celery, chopped fine
4 tbsp. finely chopped pimiento

a. Stir gelatine into 1/2 cup milk to soften
b. Beat egg yolks, remaining 3 cups milk, salt and pepper together; add to gelatine mixture.
c. Place over low heat, stirring constantly until gelatine is dissolved. (Mixture should barely come to boil.)
d. Remove from heat. Chill mixture to unbeaten egg white consistency.
e. Combine tuna, mustard, lemon juice, celery and pimiento. Fold into gelatine mixture.
f. Turn into 6-cup mold. Chill until firm.
g. Unmold. Cover with chaud froid sauce & decorate.

VIII

DESSERTS

MINIATURE PECAN TARTS

Crust

1 - 3 oz. pkg. cream cheese
1/2 cup butter or margarine
1 cup sifted all-purpose flour

Let cream cheese and butter soften at room temperature, then blend thoroughly. Stir in flour. Chill slightly, about 1 hour. Shape into 2 doz. 1" balls; place into tiny ungreased 1 3/4" muffin pans. Press dough on bottom and around sides of pans.

Filling

1/2 cup brown sugar
1/2 teas. vanilla
1/2 cup coarsely broken pecans, divided
1 1/2 teas. soft butter or margarine
Dash of salt
1/2 slightly beaten egg

Beat together, egg, sugar, butter, vanilla and salt until smooth. Divide 1/4 cup pecans among the pastry lined pans; add egg mixture and top with remaining pecans. Bake in slow oven (325°F) 25 minutes or until filling is set.

Cool. Remove from pans.

STRAWBERRY GLACE' TARTS

Crust

1 1/2 cups all-purpose flour
3/4 teas. salt
1/2 cup + 2 tbsp. Crisco
3 tbsp. water

a. Measure flour by dip-level-pour method. Mix flour & salt in bowl. Cut in shortening with pastry blender until particles are size of peas.
b. Sprinkle with water, 1 tbsp. at a time, mixing with fork until flour is moistened. Gather dough together with fingers so it cleans bowl.
c. Divide in half and form into two long rolls, about 1" in diameter. Cut rolls into 1" long pieces, then shape these pieces into balls. (Should make 24 pieces.) Roll each out into a flat circle, or oblong (depending upon shape of tart pans).
d. Line 24 tiny tart pans with pastry. Prick bottom of each with fork.
e. Bake at 450°F (very hot) 8 to 10 minutes. Remove from pan while still slightly warm. Let cool before filling.

Filling

- 1 pt. strawberries, fresh or frozen
- 1/2 cup water
- 1/2 cup granulated sugar
- 1 1/2 tbsp. corn starch
- 1 - 3 oz. pkg. cream cheese, softened, then beaten with lemon juice or vanilla.

Wash, drain and hull strawberries, if fresh. If frozen, thaw and drain. Simmer 1/2 cup crushed strawberries and 1/3 cup water about 2 1/2 minutes. Blend sugar, corn starch and remaining water; add to boiling mixture.

If desired, add a few drops of Watermelon liquid food coloring at this time. Boil 1 minute, stirring constantly. Cool. Squeeze a thin layer of cream cheese over bottom of tart shell by going 'round and 'round with a #8 decorating tube.

Place the whole, uncooked berries into the 24 tart shells. Do not fill quite to rim of shell. Cover tarts with cooked mixture. Cool. Refrigerate until firm, about 2 hours. To serve, squeeze a rosette of sweetened whipped cream or Dream Whip on top, using a pastry bag and a #32 decorating tube. These strawberry tarts may be placed back into the refrigerator until serving time.

BAVARIAN CREAM
(6 servings)

1 envelope Knox unflavored gelatine
1/2 cup granulated sugar, divided
1/8 teas. salt
2 eggs, separated
1 1/4 cups milk
1/2 teas. vanilla
1 cup heavy cream, whipped

a. Mix gelatine, 1/4 cup of the sugar & salt thoroughly in top of double boiler.
b. Beat egg yolks & milk together. Add to gelatine mixture.
c. Cook over boiling water, stirring constantly until gelatine is dissolved, about 5 minutes.
d. Remove from heat and stir in vanilla. Chill mixture to unbeaten egg white consistency.
e. Beat egg whites until stiff. Beat in remaining 1/4 cup of sugar.
f. Fold gelatine mixture into stiffly beaten egg whites.
g. Fold whipped cream into gelatine mixture.
h. Turn into 4-cup mold and chill until firm.
i. Unmold on serving plate and garnish with fresh fruit.

VARIATION ON RECIPE:

For Coffee Bavarian, in Step "a", add 2 tbsp. instant coffee to gelatine & sugar mixture.

FRUIT JELLO MOLD

(12 generous servings)

1 - 29 oz. jar Del Monte Fruits for Salad
2 - 6 oz. pkgs. Mixed Fruit Jello
1 envelope (1 tbsp.) Knox unflavored gelatine

a. Drain fruit in sieve. Should yield 1 1/2 cups juice. Chill fruit and juice separately.
b. Mix Jello and gelatine together. Pour into 3 1/2 cups boiling water and stir until dissolved.
c. Add juice to mixture and chill for about an hour. (Place Wilton 9" Petal Pan into refrigerator at this time to chill also.)
d. For design shown below: Cut in half, 4 cherries and 4 pineapple pieces. Slice in half, 4 pear pieces and 4 peach pieces.
e. Pour enough of the Jello mixture into pan to barely cover bottom. Chill until firm.
f. Remove pan from refrigerator. Press one whole cherry down into center of Jello. Press 1 peach piece down in each scallop on outside rim of pan and 1/2 cherry inside each peach.
   Press pear pieces in between peach pieces with small ends going towards center. Press circle

of pineapple pieces around center cherry. Drop spoonfuls of Jello mixture over design and chill until firm.
g. Cut remaining fruit into small pieces. Add this and 2 cups cold water to Jello mixture and chill until slightly thicker than unbeaten egg whites. (Mixture will dribble unevenly from spoon.)
h. Pour mixture over design in mold and chill for at least 2 hours. (There will be about 1/2 cup of the mixture left over...just enough for you to sample!)
i. Unmold on serving tray. (To unmold, see "Gelatine Salads & Aspics".)

TO SERVE: Use a 14" pastry bag and a #6 open star pastry tube and squeeze large shells of whipped cream or any desired topping around base of mold on serving tray.

PETITS FOURS
Daintiest of all dainty cakes!

There are two basic types of petits fours - filled and unfilled. After that, classification is impossible. There's just no limit on shapes, colors or decorations you can create. Always keep them small and dainty and use pastel colored icing along with chocolate. And, always use a paper petit four cup for each cake.

Start with your favorite pound cake recipe (or a pound cake mix) and bake in 8" x 8" x 2" square pans. Line bottom and sides with paper (after greasing. Side lining should be about 3" high. Place batter in pan to a depth of about 1 1/2". When cakes are baked, trim off top, if mounded. After cake is completely cooled, refrigerate for at least one hour before cutting into shapes.

a. Cut cake into slices 3/4" thick.

b. Trim crusts.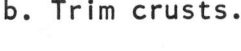

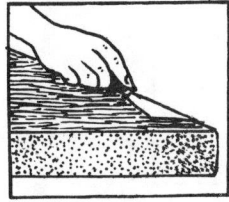 

c. Cut lengthwise through center.

d. Cut the 2 strips across into equal sections, making square shapes.......

and/or.....

e. Place the two trimmed and cut strips next to each other, but off-set them slightly and cut at an angle. Each cut should be the same width as the strips. This makes diamond shapes.

For a variety of shapes, take an untrimmed 3/4" slice and cut with small cutters.

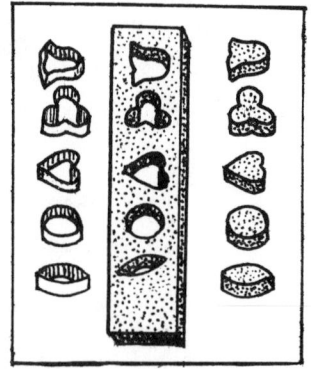

Put all cutout shapes (squares, diamonds, etc.) on tray, cover with plastic wrap and place in refrigerator for at least 2 hours (or in freezer for about 1 hour) while preparing fondant icing. (Recipe next page)

Filled Petits Fours

Cut pound cake into slices 3/4" thick, as before, then cut these slices in half, making 3/8" strips. Spread one strip with filling of either jelly, jam or buttercream icing. Assemble slices. Chill and cut into different shapes as was done with unfilled petits fours.

o o o o o o o

Before icing petits fours, coat with apricot glaze. Use pastry brush to apply glaze on top and around sides. Recipe follows.

Apricot Glaze

16 oz. apricot jam
1 tbsp. lemon juice
4 tbsp. water

Mix ingredients together in saucepan. Bring to boil. Reduce heat & simmer for 5 minutes. Press mixture through sieve, then back into saucepan to boil gently for 5 minutes. Cool, then store in a screw top jar.

Glaze is easier to apply if cakes are thoroughly chilled.

ICING PETITS FOURS

Fondant is traditionally used to ice Petits Fours. You can make it from scratch or use "Instant" fondant. In either case, the basic fondant is slightly modified for pouring over the little cakes. Recipes for "instant" fondant and fondant from scratch follow:

Instant Fondant

Mix 1/4 cup hot water to one pound of instant fondant.

Place on low heat and stir constantly with wooden spoon until fondant is smooth. This is the basic fondant.

<u>For icing Petits Fours</u>, add the following ingredients per pound of instant fondant: 2 tbsp. clear Karo syrup and 3 tbsp. butter. Stir and reheat over double boiler. Add just enough water to make consistency like Karo syrup at room temperature.

At this point, flavoring and coloring can be added. For each separate color or flavor, use a different pot and stir in until evenly blended. It can now be poured over petits fours. (Directions for pouring follow recipe for scratch fondant.)

Fondant may be reheated during pouring, or at a later date. In either case, however, a bit more water may have to be added to get the proper consistency.

Store fondant in airtight container in refrigerator.

(3 lbs. instant fondant will ice approximately 200 petits fours.)

<u>Recipe for Fondant from Scratch</u>:

For this basic fondant, you'll need either a marble slab or a sheet pan & rack and a 3" paint scraper or candy scraper. Have these handy while making the fondant.

4 cups granulated sugar
2 cups water
2 tbsp. clear Karo syrup

In a 2-quart saucepan (<u>not</u> aluminum), combine all ingredients. Stir mixture at beginning of cooking to be sure sugar is dissolved before reaching the boiling point. Cook to 238°F (high altitude) or 240°F (low altitude). Use small pastry brush dipped in hot water to wipe around pan at level of syrup to keep crystals from forming.

When mixture has reached 238°F or 240°F, remove from heat and let stand a minute until bubbles subside.

Pour out on marble slab or sheet pan setting on rack. Pour <u>away</u> from you and <u>do not</u> scrape pan.

Let set until little wrinkles appear around edges of fondant. This indicates it is cooling. When outside edges are almost cool and center is lukewarm, fondant is ready to be worked. Depending upon room temperature, should take a little less than 30 minutes.

Use paint or candy scraper and work the fondant by lifting edges and turning over towards center all around the whole amount. Keep repeating this, going 'round and 'round the fondant until it turns into a semi-solid mass. Takes about 8-10 minutes. Knead with hands until creamy and soft. Store in plastic bag at room temperature for several days, or refrigerator for several months.

NOW, to adapt the fondant to a pouring consistency for coating petits fours, do the following:

For about 50 petits fours, place 2 cups prepared fondant into top of double boiler. Set into bottom with water over low heat. Stir constantly with wooden spoon. Add 3 or 4 teaspoons water and small amount of whatever color you wish. Use liquid food coloring, <u>not</u> paste. Also add flavoring at this time, about 1 teaspoon.

Place small cakes on rack over sheet pan and pour, or spoon, fondant over them. Watch that you don't miss corners and/or portions of sides. If so, go back and mend with small spatula dipped in fondant.

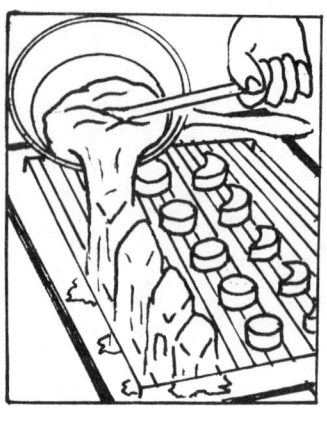

Fondant that drops into pan underneath rack can be scraped up and put back into cooking pan. (Watch for crumbs while doing this. Remove any before putting back into pan.)

After cakes have set up for 15 to 20 minutes, make sure fondant in pan is 105°F again and add a bit of water to make right consistency for pouring, then pour over cakes again. Let set for at least 20 minutes before decorating.

DECORATING PETITS FOURS

These little cakes may be decorated with various types of materials, the simplest of which would be candied fruits & nuts. Fondant or summer coating also can be used to make lines & dots. For a fancier type of decoration, buttercream or royal icing can be used to make little flowers and leaves with or without stems.

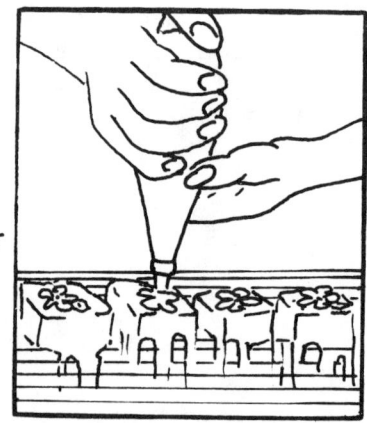

For making decorations, use Decorating Tube No. 2 for lines & dots, Tube No. 3 for stems, Nos. 65 & 67 for leaves and for Drop Flowers, Tubes such as No. 129, 224 or 225.

CREAM HORNS

Things Needed:

    1 pkg. Pepperidge Farms Frozen Puff Pastry
    1 egg
    Raspberry or black currant jam
    1 pint whipping cream
    Powdered sugar
    Cream Horn Molds

       Makes approx. 24 Cream Horns

a. Thaw pastry according to directions on box.
b. Keep one sheet in refrigerator while working with the other. (There are two 10" x 10" sheets in pkg.)
c. Roll pastry out on a lightly floured board to 16" long. (10" wide)
d. Beat one egg and brush over rolled out pastry.
e. Use pizza cutter to cut 3/4" x 16" strips.

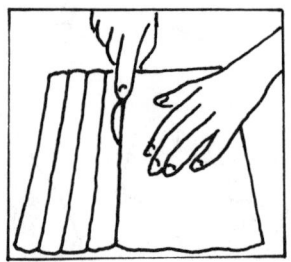 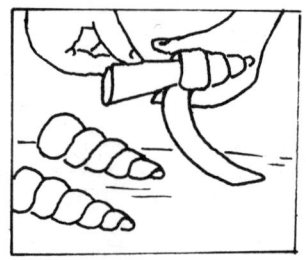

f. Wind each pastry strip around a horn mold, starting at the tip, with the <u>glazed side of the pastry outside</u>. Overlap each turn by about 1/8". As it rises during baking, the pastry will reach just short of the metal rim of mold. Set moist pastries on a baking sheet (ungreased) with the seam where the strip ends, facing downward. NOTE: Do not allow egg to get under horn on mold. Makes pastry stick to mold.

   (If you are working with only 8 molds, refrigerate rolled out strips while baking 8 horns. Pastry MUST be kept cold.)

g. Bake in center of preheated oven at 375°F about 15-20 minutes or until horns are a golden color.
h. Let cool a few minutes, then with one hand, grip the rim of mold with a clean cloth and carefully twist the mold. Hold the horn lightly in the other hand and ease it off the mold.
i. Let the horns cool completely, then put a teaspoon of jam into the end of each.
j. Just before serving time, whip the cream and spoon into horns. Or, use a pastry bag with a #22 decorating tube and squeeze into horns.
k. Dust with powdered sugar and if desired, place one-half maraschino cherry into end.

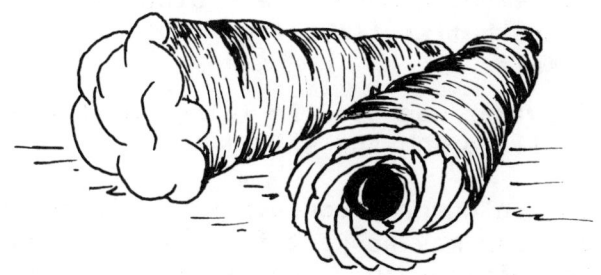

BUTTERCREAM ICING

(For decorating only)

    1 1/4 cup Crisco (or 1/2 Crisco & 1/2 butter)
    1 lb. powdered sugar
    3 tbsp. water

a. Whip Crisco at high speed until fluffy.

b. Add 1/2 of the pow. sugar. Mix at low speed until blended.

c. Add water and mix at low speed until blended. Add flavorings at this time.*

d. Mix at medium speed until thoroughly blended.

e. Add balance of pow. sugar, then whip at high speed until fluffy.

*Flavoring and Storing Buttercream

  1 teas. clear vanilla (keeps icing white)
  1/2 teas. lemon, almond or any other desired flavor.
  1 or 2 drops butter flavoring
  Pinch of salt

  NOTE: If butter was used in icing, omit the butter flavoring and salt.

Store icing in covered container. This decorating buttercream may be kept for weeks, or months, in the refrigerator. Return to room temperature to rewhip to proper consistency.

ROYAL ICING

1 lb. powdered sugar
1/4 cup meringue powder
1/2 cup water (tap, not warm)

a. Mix pow. sugar and meringue powder until blended.

b. Add water and mix at low speed until blended.

c. Mix at high speed until fluffy.

NOTE: If using portable electric mixer, it's best to mix only one-half batch at a time.

Keep this icing covered at all times with damp cloth or tight fitting lid. It crusts over very quickly.

If climate is damp or humid, short the water by 2 teaspoons.

<u>Do</u> <u>not</u> store royal icing in refrigerator. Keep at room temperature. It can be rewhipped as long as three weeks after being made.

<u>Do</u> <u>not</u> let any grease come in contact with royal icing. Icing will fall like an angel food cake!

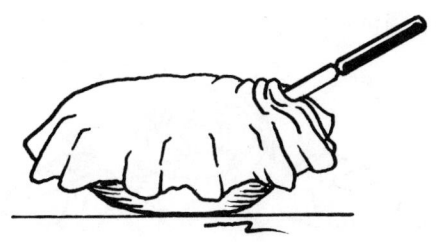

CREAM CHEESE MINTS

8 oz. cream cheese
2 lbs. powdered sugar
7 to 9 drops flavoring <u>oil</u>

Mix all ingredients together. Knead with hands until it resembles pie dough. Roll into small balls. Dip in granulated sugar (this keeps it from sticking to the molds). Press into desired mold. Pop out immediately.

Makes approximately 200 mints.

Can be eaten immediately or, if stored in covered container, will keep indefinitely in refrigerator.

Mints can be colored by using paste food coloring. (Liquid coloring makes the mints sticky and gooey.) Simply knead the paste coloring into the amount of mixture you wish to color.

UNCOOKED BUTTER FONDANT MINTS

1 egg white
2 1/2 cups sifted powdered sugar
1 tbsp. butter, softened
1/2 teas. flavoring <u>oil</u>

Combine ingredients and mix until creamy. Follow procedure for molding Cream Cheese mints. These mints can be placed in an airtight container and frozen for up to 2 months.

Makes 11 oz. of mixture, enough for approximately 60 mints of assorted sizes in mint molds.

HOW TO USE A DECORATING BAG COUPLER

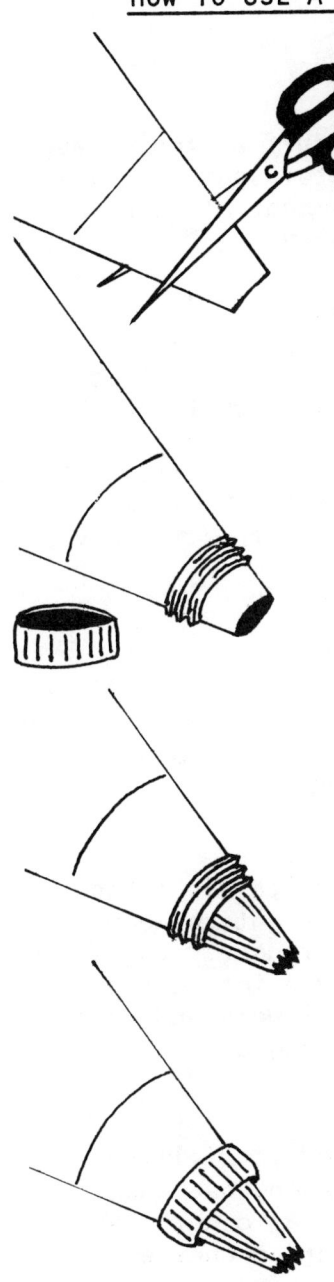

Cut off tip of bag, far enough so several threads on coupler will show when pushed through hole. Start by cutting off approximately 3/4". However, be careful how much you cut off at first. If hole is too large, coupler will fall through and bag is ruined.

Twist ring off coupler. Set aside. Drop coupler into bag. Push down with table knife to see how many threads show. If none, or only one shows, remove coupler and cut off again. Repeat until at least two or three threads show.

Place decorating tube over end of coupler.

Hold tube in place as you twist ring on to secure it.

If you wish to use a different decorating tube on the same bag of icing, simply twist ring off, change tube and twist ring on again.

HOW TO FILL AND USE A DECORATING BAG

Fold down a wide cuff at top of bag. Using a narrow metal spatula, pick up only a small amount of icing at a time to fill bag.*

Place these small amounts into the bag, starting right down in the bottom, pressing the spatula against the side of the bag each time to scrape off the icing. Do this until the level of icing is about two-thirds the way up the side of bag.

Twist top of bag tightly down to level of icing, then

grasp twisted bag with right hand, holding the twist tight between the thumb and forefinger. Bag is to be held at 45° angle for most purposes. For drop flowers and stars, hold at 90° angle.

* Use the same method for filling and using a decorating bag when working with material other than icing, such as a cream cheese mixture, whipped cream, etc.

Summer Coating

If you want to add a bit of sweets to a buffet table, and do not wish to go into some fancy type of pastries or petit fours, Summer Coating is the answer. You can make a variety of candies, such as bark, clusters, mints, fancy molded chocolates and other goodies to serve in a bon bon dish. Solves the "sweets" problem and it's simply a matter of melting the Summer Coating to make mints & molds, or adding nutmeats, dates, etc., to make delicious candies!

WHAT IS SUMMER COATING?

Summer Coating is perhaps the most versatile of all candy products and is often (but erroneously) referred to as White Chocolate. It comes in a variety of colors, such as White, Pink, Green, Yellow, Orchid, Blue, Red, Orange and Peach. (All have the same flavor: a light vanilla.) Also Butterscotch and Peanut Butter, both a light tan. Also, a Dark and Light chocolate. Some are in wafer form and are not to be confused with the "White Chocolate" (white & dark chocolate slabs, found in super markets & drug stores). Check with your local supplier or favorite mail order house for Summer Coating wafers.

It might be well to note here that Summer Coating also is not to be confused with Milk Chocolate, which comes in slabs, bricks or wafers, and has to be "tempered", requiring exact temperature and humidity readings.

Summer Coating is usually sold in one and two pound packages. There are approximately 224 wafers per pound. The Coating keeps indefinitely when stored in a cool place. Do not store in refrigerator or let it become exposed to heat.

You'll find Summer Coating so easy to work with, it'll be like making "instant candy"!

SUPPLIES NEEDED for working with Summer Coating:

    Summer Coating   Wax Paper
    Double Boiler or   Cookie Sheet
      Electric Skillet   Wooden Spoon
    Oil Flavoring   Molds: Sugar, Candy &
                                          Mint Molds

Asst. nuts, candy chips (Peppermint, Cherry Chips, etc.), Pretzels, Dates, etc. (Depends upon the type of goodies you wish to make.)

DIRECTIONS for working with Summer Coating:

    Summer Coating wafers must be melted for making the candies described in this chapter.

    To do this, heat water to boiling in the bottom of a double boiler. Remove from fire and set top of double boiler (containing Summer Coating wafers) into bottom. Stir slowly with wooden spoon until all wafers have completely melted. (If using electric skillet, set dial on warm or under 100°F. Stir with wooden spoon until melted.)

    DO NOT COOK COATING OVER DIRECT FIRE OR ALLOW MOISTURE INTO IT. Either will ruin it!

    TO FLAVOR Summer Coating, use Oil Flavors only! Alcohol or water based flavors will not blend with the coating. Takes about 12 drops (a scant 1/8 teas.) Oil Flavoring to flavor 1/2 lb. (approx. 112 wafers).

    White Summer Coating may be colored with the use of a special powdered "candy color", available in many cake and food decorating supply shoppes. DO NOT use liquid or water-based coloring. And paste color is not advisable because it does not blend well with the melted mixture. Actually, it isn't necessary to color coatings because they are sold in a variety of attractive colors.

SUMMER COATING CAN BE RE-MELTED & USED OVER....

If you still have some melted Summer Coating left over, pour it out on wax paper, let set, then store in plastic bag. It can be broken into pieces and re-melted at a later date.

MOLDED DESIGNS, MINTS & MINIATURE BON BONS....

You may wish to make the Summer Coating slightly softer for making these items (described later in this chapter) by adding 1 teas. coconut oil (obtainable at health food stores) to 1 lb. of Summer Coating.

Summer Coating Candies

<u>HOW TO MAKE BARK</u>:

To pan of melted Summer Coating, add whatever ingredient and/or flavor you desire, stir, then pour onto wax papered cookie sheet, spreading thin with spoon or spatula. Let set until cool, then break into pieces. Or, just before the candy is completely set, cut into squares with pizza cutter.

APPROXIMATE YIELD from 1/2 lb. (112 wafers) Summer Coating: Adding 3/4 cup (about 3 oz.) coarsely chopped nuts to the Coating will make a thin spread of approx. 8" x 10". This can be broken into various size pieces or, cut with pizza cutter into 80 1-inch squares. Can be cut into larger squares if desired, with a smaller yield.

Some SUGGESTED COMBINATIONS ARE:

NUT BARK...Use any kind of nuts (Almonds, Cashews, Pecans, etc.) and White or Chocolate Summer Coating.

PEPPERMINT BARK...Mix about 1/2 cup Peppermint Chips into Pink or Green Coating. For extra color, sprinkle chips on top of Coating after pouring and spreading out on cookie sheet.

MAPLE BARK...Mix 3/4 cup chopped pecans and 2 heaping tablespoons Maple Chips into 1/2 lb. Butterscotch Coating.

CHERRY BARK...Mix Cherry Chips and Pink Coating with any desired nut meats.

HOW TO MAKE CLUSTERS:

Stir nuts, dates and/or raisins into color Coating of your choice. Add larger amount of the combination of these ingredients than used for Bark, I.e. about 1 1/4 cup, instead of 3/4 cup, to 1/2 lb. Coating.

Let complete mixture cool down until a bit thick, then spoon onto waxed paper cookie sheet in little mounds. 1/2 lb. Coating with ingredients should yield approx. 30 clusters. (The yield depends upon the size of the mounds.)

RICE KRISPIE CLUSTERS...Mix 1 3/4 cups Rice Krispies (or other dry breakfast cereal) into 1/2 lb. White Summer Coating (white works best, since the Krispies seem to discolor other Coating). Let cool until slightly thick, then spoon onto wax paper. Makes about 24 medium size clusters, approx. 2" across and 5/8" high. (Again, number of Clusters depends upon size of mounds.)

HOW TO MAKE CANDY PRETZELS:

Use the small, thin twisted pretzels, and dip into melted Coating, covering well. Remove each pretzel individually, shake lightly to remove excess Coating. Place on wax papered cookie sheet to dry.

For a variety, make White, Pink, Green and Chocolate pretzels.

Summer Coating Molds

There is a very large variety of molds that can be used to make beautiful designs with Summer Coating. Any plastic sugar molds are suitable...and there are many, many designs for various holidays in these molds...Easter, Halloween, Christmas, etc., as well as numerous designs for almost any occasion. Also, lots of candy molds are available, as well as a myriad of designs in mint molds. There are even Summer Coating Lollipop molds!

GENERAL DIRECTIONS FOR MOLDING SUMMER COATING:

Pour, or spoon, melted Summer Coating into mold. Lift mold up, then tap against table several times to bring any air bubbles to the top. Place in refrigerator until set. Setting time depends upon size and depth of mold.

Remove mold from refrigerator, turn upside down over wax paper and tap lightly until Coating design drops out. If using flexible mint molds, designs can be pushed out from back of molds.

HOW TO MAKE MINTS:

Flavor melted Summer Coating with Oil Flavors as mentioned previously....such as Peppermint for pink, Wintergreen for green, Lemon for yellow, etc. (When making mints with Summer Coating, use a whole sheet of molds, not just single molds as are used for cream cheese mints.)

Spoon Coating into molds, then proceed as explained under "General Directions".

The number of mints obtained from Summer Coating depends upon size of the mold used. An overall average, however, would be approx. 80 mints from 1 lb. of Coating.

HOW TO MAKE MINIATURE BON BONS:

Use light or dark chocolate Summer Coating and the 25-cavity Fruit & Flower mold. Proceed as for mints.

1 lb. Summer Coating will yield approx. 95 bon bons, made with the Fruit & Flower mold.

Marzipan
A Most Elite Confection!

Marzipan is possibly the richest and most elegant food in the category of sweets. Any book having to do with fancy and creative foods would not be complete without at least an introduction to this marvelous confection.

Working with Marzipan is as easy as working with modeling clay. It can be molded into everything--- from fruits & vegetables to the delicate petals of a beautiful rose. You can cut it into any shape desired and for any occasion---whether it be hearts for Valentine's Day, shamrocks for St. Patrick's, chicks and bunnies for Easter, or witches for Halloween - simply by using cookie cutters.

Miniature Marzipan fruits have long been an almost universal tradition at Thanksgiving and Christmas and have a multiplicity of uses. They can be boxed like candy for gifts, served in party dishes for guests, used on cake tops and around the base of cakes, wrapped separately (or in bunches) in plastic with a ribbon bow and hung on the Christmas tree.

And remember: Marzipan can be molded months ahead, placed in airtight containers and refrigerated indefinitely.

Most super markets carry ready-to-use Marzipan in 7 oz. packages. If you prefer to make your own, a recipe follows. In either case, you will find that working with Marzipan is truly a fun venture!

MARZIPAN RECIPE

1 cup (8 oz.can) Almond Paste (or 7 oz. pkg. OK)
2 1/4 cups Powdered Sugar, sifted
1 egg white
2 tbsp. white Karo syrup

a. Break almond paste into small pieces by hand in large mixing bowl.
b. Add pow. sugar & mix by hand until mixture is like small beads.
c. Add egg whites & Karo & knead in bowl until mixture is a solid mass.
d. Remove to a board lightly covered with pow. sugar & knead until smooth. (Should be the consistency of pie dough. If it seems too soft, knead in more pow. sugar.)
e. Place in plastic bag & tie. Keep tightly covered at all times.

Makes approx. 1 lb. 4 oz. (20 oz.) Marzipan.
Fruit yield in 20 oz., approx. 50 (.375 oz. ea.)

NOTE: To substitute meringue powder for egg whites, use 2 teas. mer. pow. (mixed thoroughly with the pow. sugar) and 2 1/2 teas. water. Add water & Karo at the same time. (Marzipan made with meringue powder will keep indefinitely in the refrigerator.)

MATERIALS NEEDED FOR MAKING MARZIPAN FRUITS:

Marzipan
Round Toothpicks
Orange stick
   (with pointed end)
Paring Knife
Sm. Artist's Brush
Cotton Swabs
Marzipan Leaves
   Oil Flavoring (optional)

Nutmeg Grater
   (smallest design on
   regular grater)
#5 cake decorating tube
Sponge
Egg Whites
Whole Cloves
Paste Food Coloring

For making MARZIPAN VEGETABLES, add the following materials:

#2 cake decorating tube
Cocoa

Sm. Sieve (1/16" gauge mesh)
Soft Pastry Brush

COLORING MARZIPAN

To determine how much colored marzipan you'll need to make a quantity of the same fruit, such as a dozen peaches, make a ball of marzipan about 2 1/2" in diameter. Place this on a board or counter lightly covered with powdered sugar and use to make a roll 3/4" in diameter. Form the roll with the palms of your hands, not your fingertips. (Keeps it more uniform.)

Measure with ruler & cut off a 12" piece of the roll, then a 1" piece, separately. Make a "wad" of the 12" piece and place both pieces in a plastic bag & tie. Place scrap leftover roll back with the rest of the recipe in another plastic bag.

(See "Guide for Making Marzipan Fruits & Vegetables" in this chapter for complete instructions on sizes and coloring.)

Color the marzipan before molding the fruit. For example, to color the wad of marzipan mentioned above for peaches, knead a large amount of Lemon Yellow paste coloring into the 1" piece first. To do this, press a fingertip into it to make an indentation, put coloring into this, then a teaspoon of powdered sugar over the coloring. Stand over the sink to knead the coloring and sugar. Wash hands thoroughly before starting to color the wad.

Pinch off about half the small colored piece and knead into the larger wad. Keep adding bits of the concentrated colored marzipan, kneading thoroughly, until you have the desired shade. If, after using all the concentrated color, the larger piece is still not the shade you want, pinch off a small piece and add coloring & powdered sugar to make another dark shade, then keep kneading bits of it into the wad. <u>Do not</u> add paste coloring directly to the amount of marzipan you wish to color because (1) there's a good chance you might add too much coloring, making it necessary to add more marzipan to lighten the shade and ending up with much more of the color than you need and (2) it is difficult to knead pure paste coloring into marzipan without getting light and dark spots.

<u>PLEASE</u> <u>NOTE</u>: If you are making a variety of fruit, such as a dozen each of apples, peaches, bananas, oranges, etc., start coloring the pale yellow for peaches first, then deep yellow for bananas, then orange and last, the red. If you work with red first, some coloring will come off on the yellow marzipan despite how good you wash your hands. In other words, use light colors before darker ones.

The same rule applies to molding the fruit: Mold the pale yellow peaches & pears first, then the deep yellow lemons, bananas, etc.

(The "Guide....", mentioned previously, gives the order in which the marzipan is to be colored & molded.)

Some of the fruit & vegetables require a tint of extra color after being molded. For those that need a shaded tint, such as peaches, pears, etc., use cotton swabs to apply coloring diluted with water. Use the small artist's brush to paint stripes or dots where called for, such as on bananas & pineapples. This is explained in detail in "Molding the Fruit & Vegetables".

FLAVORING MARZIPAN

Use <u>oil flavoring</u> <u>only</u>. Marzipan is delicious without flavoring, but for making fruits, a little flavor adds a realistic taste. After marzipan is colored, knead in a few drops of oil flavor, such as orange oil for oranges, strawberry oil for strawberries, etc. Taste the flavored marzipan, then add more flavoring if needed. Oils are much stronger than regular flavoring or extracts, so be careful!

ASSEMBLY LINE MARZIPAN FRUITS

Using peaches again for an example, form the pale yellow colored marzipan into a 3/4" roll again. Place a ruler next to the roll and, with a paring knife, cut roll into 1" pieces. Place these pieces into a plastic bag & tie, so won't dry out while molding peaches. Or, instead of a tie-tie, a clothespin to fasten the bag will make it quicker to open and close!

The Guide on the following pages gives the coloring, size, yield, weight & tint for making the fruit & vegetables, as well as a basis to go on for determining how much marzipan to make for a specified number.

For example, if you want to make a dozen each peaches, pears, bananas, pineapples, oranges, apples & strawberries, multiply .375 oz. x 84 (7 doz.), which equals 31.5 ozs. 1 1/2 batches (30 ozs.) marzipan should be sufficient. (Marzipan recipe actually makes slightly over the 20 ozs. stated.)

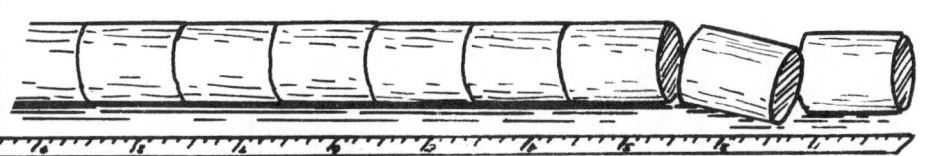

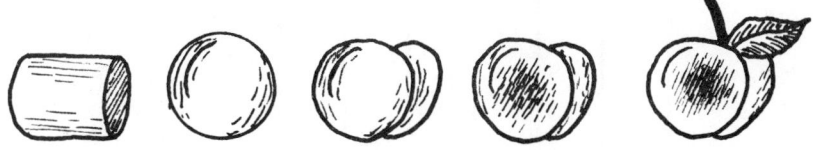

Guide for Making Marzipan Fruits & Vegetables

ITEM	COLOR MARZIPAN	ROLL DIAM.	LENGTH	YIELD	WEIGHT	TINT
Peach	Pale Yellow	3/4"	1"	1	.375 oz.	Pink on each side
Pear	"	"	"	"	"	Pink on one side
Lemon	Deep Yellow	"	"	"	"	Pale green on ends
Banana	"	"	"	"	"	Brown
Pineapple	"	"	"	"	"	Green, brown & pink
Orange	Orange	"	"	"	"	-----
Apple	Red	"	"	"	"	-----
Strawberry	"	"	"	"	"	-----

ITEM	COLOR MARZIPAN	ROLL DIAM.	LENGTH	YIELD	WEIGHT	TINT
Cherries)--Mold--- Leaves)	(Red----------- (Green---------	3/4"----- " -----	1/2") ")	1	.375 oz.	---Brown on stem
Grapes)----Mold--- Leaves)	(Purple-------- (Green---------	" ----- " -----	") ")	"	"	----Brown on stem
Plum	Royal Blue	"	1"	"	"	Violet on ea. side
Carrot) ------ " Leaves)	(Orange-------- (Green---------	" ----- 3/8"-----	") 1/2")	"	.45 oz.	-----
Corn) ------ " Husks)	(Deep Yellow-- (Pale Green----	3/4"---- 3/8"----	1") 1/2")	"	.45 oz.	-----
Tomato	Red	3/4"	1"	"	.375	-----
Pepper	Deep Green	"	"	"	"	-----
Potato	None	"	"	"	"	Cocoa only/no tint

MOLDING THE FRUIT

Each piece of fruit is first molded into a ball, without creases on the surface of the marzipan. To do this, take a piece of marzipan out of the plastic bag & knead between fingers until surface is smooth, then roll into a ball between the palms of your hands (Fig. a).

NOTE: Most molding of marzipan is done with the palms or side of the hands. If fingertips are used for molding, they leave indentations.

Fig. a.

Remember to use the same sequence to mold the fruit as you did to color the marzipan--pale yellow, deep yellow, etc.

PEACHES: Roll marzipan piece into ball, flatten slightly with fingertip on top, then use toothpick to make indentation in one side from top to bottom. Use cotton swab to tint pink blush on each side, then attach leaf.*

*Leaves are described later on. Whether you are using "store bought" leaves or making your own, they should be pressed against a sponge soaked in egg white before sticking into fruit. Egg white acts as a glue.

PEARS: Mold ball into teardrop shape with sides of palms (Fig. b), then curve slightly. Tint with pink on one side. Stick clove stem in top and clove bud in bottom. Be sure to wet clove in egg white.

Fig. b.

LEMONS: Mold ball into oval shape, pinch ends to a point with fingertips. Roll lemon over grater, then tint ends a very pale green. Stick clove bud in one end.

BANANAS: Mold ball into long oval shape, with blunt points at each end. With shape setting on board, press between top two joints of forefingers (Fig. c) on three sides to make a "squared" look. (The fourth side will automatically fall into the same shape.) Curve slightly.

Fig. c.

With small artist's brush, paint thin brown stripes down each squared corner & a wide band around one end. Press brush on damp cloth to remove excess liquid, then lightly brush over a few portions of banana with splotches of brown. Tint other end pale green.

PINEAPPLES: Mold ball into egg shape (smaller at one end). Press toothpick diagonally across shape several times, then criss-cross lines over this. Use #5 tube to press into each diamond shape made by the lines. Tint whole pineapple pale green, using swab. Paint thin brown stripes down lines with small brush. Use swab to dot each circle with pink. Insert spear top.

ORANGES: Roll ball over grater, then insert clove into orange with only the bud showing.

APPLES: Mold ball slightly smaller on bottom, make indentation in top with orange stick, small indentations around this with toothpick, then stick leaf on.

STRAWBERRIES: Mold ball into shape of apple (smaller at one end), then flatten small end slightly. Roll over grater, then insert leaf.

CHERRIES & GRAPES: Both of these can be made easily with molds, instead of spending a lot of time hand-molding such small items with so many separate pieces. They're both on a 25-cavity sheet of mint molds, called "Fruit & Flower Mold". (Check with your local supply store or favorite mail order house.)

To make the Cherries: Divide the piece of red marzipan in half, roll into two balls, then press into mold. Roll green marzipan into ball, dampen small spot with egg white, press into leaf & stem portion of mold with dampened spot next to cherries. Turn the mold over and press to pop the cherries out. Use brush to paint stem brown.

To make the Grapes: Use the mold that has five grapes & a leaf (there are two grape molds on the sheet). Press small ball of green marzipan into the leaf & stem portion. Put a little egg white on side next to grapes. Press a ball of purple (Violet & Baker's Rose combined) into the grape portion, then pop out as before. Paint the stem brown.

PLUMS: Mold ball into oval shape, then make indentation with toothpick from top to bottom (like peach). Tint each side with Violet coloring, then attach leaf.

CARROT: Mold ball into long oval shape, smaller at one end. Use toothpick to make slightly indented lines across carrot. Brush over lines with very light brown, using small artist's brush. Cut a 3/4" end off round toothpick; stick cut end into carrot.

CARROT LEAVES: Roll marzipan into ball. Press ball through sieve (1/16" gauge mesh). Scrape off with point of knife, then push down on pointed end of toothpick.

CORN: Mold ball into long oval shape, slightly smaller at one end. Mark criss-cross lines on shape with paring knife to make kernels.

CORN HUSKS: Mold balls into tear drop shape. Roll flat, keeping sharp point on one end. Make two indentations with toothpick, then attach to corn, turning each end out to a curve.

TOMATO: Press ball down slightly in center. Make indentations around top with toothpick, then insert clove stem into center.

PEPPER: Mold ball slightly smaller at bottom. Use #2 tube to make deep hole in top, then toothpick to make deep indentations (4 or 5) around sides.

POTATO: Mold ball into elongated shape. Do not try to make it exactly symetrical. Make a couple of indentations with fingertips and/or curve it slightly. Use #2 tube to press little "eyes" all over potato. Mix about half & half cocoa and powdered sugar (or use ready prepared cocoa mix). Brush this all over potato with soft pastry brush. (If potato is dipped into cocoa, then brushed off, takes more time and too much cocoa clings to potato!)

LEAVES FOR MARZIPAN FRUIT

<u>Ready made leaves</u> for marzipan fruit are available in coated paper or plastic--check your local supply store or mail order house.

These leaves come in three shapes:

<u>Regular</u> - to be used for peaches, plums & apples.

<u>Strawberry</u>

<u>Misc.</u> - to be used for pineapples.

Cut stems off. Cut one leaf to a spear shape for inserting into top of pineapple.

o o o o o o o o o o o o o o o o o o o o o

<u>If you prefer to make your own leaves</u> out of marzipan, the following instructions will show you how:

<u>For Peaches, Plums & Apple Leaves,</u>

(a) Roll green marzipan into a small ball, 1/4" in diameter. (b) With fingertips, mold into cone shape. (c) Flatten out on wax paper with fingertips until it's about 3/4" long, then use toothpick to make veins. Apply sponge/egg whites, then stick on fruit. Push a clove stem into fruit at bottom of leaf.

a   b   c

For Strawberry Leaves:

(a) Roll green colored marzipan into a 3/8" ball. (b) Flatten out between fingertips to a circle about 3/4" in diameter. (c) Use paring knife to cut into circle about 8 times, leaving 1/4" in center intact. (d) Pinch ends into points, place on strawberry, then make a tiny roll of green marzipan to apply down in center.

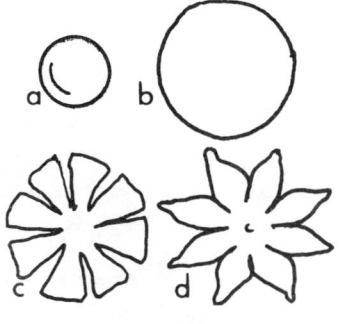

For Pineapple Spears:

(a) Make a ball 3/8" in diameter. (b) Mold into cone shape. (c) Press out to a fan shape with fingertips. (d) Cut fan to make 6 sections, leaving bottom intact. (e) Pinch ends to points, then make roll of whole fan. Use orange stick to make large hole in top of pineapple. Dip bottom of spears into sponge/egg whites, then insert into hole.

o o o o o o o o o o o o o o o o o o o o o o o

The following pages give a few examples of how marzipan can be used to make a variety of decorative pieces to set on a buffet table, to wrap for gifts or even hang on a wall for Christmas!

CHRISTMAS FRUIT WREATH

This wreath can be made on a cake top, around the base of a cake, around a large candle for a centerpiece or fruit can be mounted on a green styrofoam circle for a hanging decoration.

Note the arrangement of the fruit---five bananas are placed at equal spaces in the circle. Other fruits are placed between the bananas, with bunches of cherries & grapes filling in spaces between the larger fruits. (To make the wreath on styrofoam circle, break round toothpicks in two, push into styrofoam, then stick fruits on picks.)

CONVERSATION PIECE

Make a large apple & orange out of marzipan to set on a cheese cutting board and let guests cut their own piece of candy! Makes an attractive (and sure to be talked about) addition to any buffet table.

Mold an apple (with uncolored marzipan) from a ball about 2" in diameter. Use a 1 1/4" ball of red marzipan and roll it out on a board or counter to 1/16" thickness. Brush egg white over it with a soft pastry brush or sponge. Be sure all areas are covered.

Wrap apple by setting it upside down in center of red marzipan. Pull marzipan up around sides of apple, then trim off excess with paring knife. Smooth apple all over by rolling between palms of hands, firmly, so skin will stick to inside. Make a large green marzipan leaf and stick on top with a clove stem.

Do the same thing to make an orange, making the inside a light orange, wrapping it with a darker shade, then rolling it over a grater and sticking the clove in the top.

CANDY BOX WITH MARZIPAN FRUIT

Place fruits in bon bon cups to make beautiful boxes of marzipan for Christmas gifts. Or, combined with chocolates, makes an elegant dish of candies to serve guests.

FRUITCAKE DECORATED WITH MARZIPAN

Use a holly leaf cutter to cut leaves from green marzipan, rolled out to 1/16" thickness. Make veins with toothpick. Make lots of little 1/4" red balls for berries. Stick to top of fruitcake with very small dots of Karo syrup. Wrap in plastic and you have just made a beautiful gift!

HORN OF PLENTY WITH MARZIPAN VEGETABLES

Here's a great marzipan creation for Thanksgiving that can be used on a cake top, set on a small tray for the buffet table, or placed in a small candy box for a gift.

Color a 2 1/2" marzipan ball to a deep yellow, using Egg Yellow coloring.

a. Roll out on a board to cone shape.
b. Stand it upright, slant to one side and press around bottom.
c. Lay flat on board again.
d. Form into a curve.
e. Using round toothpick, press lines from each side & over top. Use small artist's brush & brown coloring to paint shaded portion, darker at bottom & shading off about half way up to the deep yellow. Paint end a solid brown.

Make up about 15 green marzipan leaves (as mentioned previously for peaches, plums & apples). Stick leaves and vegetables into end of horn with round toothpicks.

MARZIPAN FILLED BASKETS

     .....For Place Favors

     .....For tying on packages

     .....For hanging on Christmas trees

     .....For advertising your name or state

        Or, just for the fun of it!

Many supply stores carry these miniature woven baskets and they make great little token gifts when filled with marzipan fruits and vegetables. The baskets are 1 1/2" x 2 1/4" x 1 1/4" deep and hold about six pieces.

You don't have to label them "Idaho" Potatoes, they can be "Colorado Peaches", or... "Jones' Strawberries", or... "Smith's Potatoes", etc.,
    etc.,
        etc.

To wrap: Set in center of 12" square of plastic wrap. Gather up on top of basket & tie with narrow ribbon or string, then attach card with message. Cut off excess plastic on top.

IX

═PUNCHES═

RUBY FRUIT PUNCH

2 - 28 oz. bottles chilled ginger ale
2 tbsp. lemon juice
1 orange, thinly sliced
2 quarts chilled cranberry juice cocktail
2 cups chilled apple juice

Put ginger ale, lemon juice, and the orange slices in punch bowl. Add cranberry juice and apple juice. Stir to blend. Add a few ice cubes.

                      Makes 30 - 5 oz. servings

SPICED ORANGE PUNCH

1 cup water
2 three-inch cinnamon sticks
1/4 teas. whole cloves
2 cans (12 oz. ea.) frozen orange juice concentrate, thawed
2 bottles (28 oz. ea.) ginger ale, chilled

Bring water, cinnamon sticks and cloves to boiling in saucepan. Simmer 5 minutes. Chill. Just before serving, strain into punch bowl. Add orange juice and ginger ale. Garnish with orange peel cutouts, if desired. Pour over one ice cube in each punch cup.

                      Makes 24 - 4 oz. servings

DECORATIVE ICE PIECE FOR PUNCH BOWL

For a fancy ice piece to float in your punch bowl, choose any shape pan or mold that will fit the punch bowl, and that still leaves space around the sides. Make the design shown below in a ring pan 7" across the bottom (9" across top). The pan is 3" deep, but fill only to 1 1/2".

Use sliced oranges, sliced limes or lemons, whole maraschino cherries, grapes (seeded), whole strawberries, pineapple slices, or any fruit that will complement your punch. It is best, however, to use no more than three different fruits to make a more distinctive design.

For crystal clear ice, boil & cool water before pouring into mold.

To make ice piece: Prepare place in freezer where mold will set level. Pour very small amount of water into mold (no more than one-eighth inch). Freeze. Take out of freezer and set fruits in place on sheet of ice. Pour another very small amount of water into mold. Freeze until fruit is stuck to ice.

When everything is completely frozen, pour more water into mold (up to a depth of approximately 1 1/2") and freeze again.

To unmold, simply invert the mold and wipe it with a hot wet cloth. Be sure the ice is supported on the underside so it will not crack when it comes loose from the mold.

Carnations, roses, mums or other flowers can be frozen in the mold instead of fruit. Wash flowers, remove stems and place top side down in mold.

PINK LEMONADE PUNCH

2 cans (12 oz. ea.) frozen pink lemonade
5 cans water
2 quarts ginger ale

Chill ginger ale. Thaw lemonade & mix with water... chill. Cut several thin slices of lemon and have ice cubes ready. To serve: Pour lemonade into punch bowl, then a few ice cubes and ginger ale. Garnish with lemon slices.

Makes 30 - 5 oz. servings

CHAMPAGNE PUNCH

1 quart sauterne   )
2 cups brandy   )
2 quarts champagne   )---Chill all ingredients
1 quart sparkling water   )

Mix wine with brandy. Pour over about 10 ice cubes in punch bowl. Add champagne and sparkling water. Serve at once.

                            Makes 50 - 3 oz. servings

FRUIT PUNCH

2 cups Sugar Syrup*
Tea (3 cups tap water, 4 teas. instant tea, without sugar or lemon)
Orange juice, 3 cups (1 - 8 oz. can, frozen, 2 cans water)
Lemon juice, 1 cup (fresh or bottled reconstituted)
Pineapple juice, 3 cups (1 - 8 oz. can frozen, 2 cans water)
Ginger ale, 1 1/2 quarts (48 oz.)

Dissolve instant tea in water. Combine fruit juices, sugar syrup and tea in large container. If making the day before, pour into bottles or leave in covered container and place in refrigerator.

When ready to serve, place in punch bowl, add ginger ale and ice cubes.

                            Makes 30 - 5 oz. servings

*Sugar Syrup: Combine 1 1/3 cup granulated sugar and 1 1/3 cup water in saucepan. Stir over heat until sugar is dissolved. Bring to boiling point. Let boil without stirring about 7 minutes. Cool before mixing into punch. Makes 2 cups.

HOT APPLE CIDER PUNCH

1 gal. apple cider
2 sticks cinnamon (3 inch sticks)
2/3 cups granulated sugar
2 oranges
Whole cloves

Heat cider, cinnamon & sugar to boiling point. Cover and simmer over low heat 20 minutes. Slice oranges (unpeeled) and stick whole cloves all around edges.

Use crockpot for serving (keeps punch hot). Put several orange slices into pot, then strain punch over them. Stir. Float rest of orange slices on top.

                    Makes 24 - 4 oz. servings

X

"MEAT & POTATOES"

Looking for reception menus without frills? Do you just need <u>good</u> <u>food</u> without all the time consuming preparation usually required?

Then this is the chapter for you!

The foods here are not fancy. But they are functional.

I call it "basic catering".

When time is short, or you have no desire to create fancy decorated molds, sandwich loaves, etc., "basic foods"---like meat and potatoes---can be "dressed up" with a minimum of effort, yet presented on a buffet table at a most elegant wedding or party!

Thus, this chapter is devoted to presenting food in the most attractive way possible---even though it may be as simple as "meat and potatoes"!

If you're in the catering business, you should have at least a few menus that are less time consuming than others in this book, but which can still be made to appear attractive with some very simple basic decorating.

And it can all be done at very little expense.

Start with a basic menu of cold cuts, cheeses and potato salad, add some thinly sliced variety breads, relishes and potato chips and you have a buffet of foods everyone will like.

Potato salad can be made a day or two ahead, cold cuts and cheese can be placed on tray(s) a day ahead, wrapped in plastic and stored in refrigerator.

You can use this same menu many times over and make it look different each time, simply by changing decorations on the potato salad and arrangement of meat on trays. First of all, however, make sure the food is tasty as well as attractive. Here is a recipe for Potato Salad that should please everybody.

POTATO SALAD

8 potatoes, med. size (approx. 3 1/4 lbs.)
    (red, new potatoes are best)
1 doz. eggs, med. size
1 3/4 cups celery, chopped, loosely packed
    (approx. 1 med. size bunch)
1/2 cup green onions, chopped, loosely packed
    (8 med. size)
1/2 cup bell pepper, chopped (green or red)
    (1 small size pepper)
16 med. size black olives, pitted, chopped
16 med. size green stuffed olives, chopped
1/4 cup dill pickle, chopped
1 tbsp. + 1 teas. lemon juice (or vinegar)
3/4 cup mayonnaise
Salt & pepper to taste

                   Yield: 24 - 4 oz. servings.

Scrub potatoes & put into 4 qt. pot in hot water, unpeeled.

Bring to boil, turn heat down slightly, then cook for about 1 hr. & 20 min. (Time depends upon size of potatoes.) Stick fork in potato to test. If fork is real easy to push into center, potato is done. Set aside to cool.

- BOIL THE EGGS.....

    Put eggs into 4 qt. pot, cover with cold water & add 1/4 cup vinegar (makes peeling eggs much easier). Bring to boil, turn heat down slightly & cook for 10 minutes.

    Run cold water over eggs to cool slightly while cracking all shells. Let set for 5 minutes in cold water, then peel. Set aside.

- CHOP INGREDIENTS.....

    Chop all ingredients (except potatoes & eggs) and put into 5 qt. mixing bowl.

    Peel potatoes, then cut into four or six slices, lengthwise (depending on size), then slice crosswise.

    Set four eggs aside (for decorating top of salad) & cut remaining eight eggs into halves & slice.

    Put potatoes, eggs and mayonnaise into mixing bowl. Sprinkle salt & pepper over mixture and mix gently with wooden spoon. Taste and add more salt & pepper if needed.

- DECORATE SALAD.....

    Place the salad in a 9" x 13" x 2" container and smooth over top with spatula or back of a large spoon.

    To make this design, cut the four remaining eggs in half and remove yolks. Press whites and yolks, <u>separately</u>, through sieve with fingertips into bowls.

Mark top into sections, using a ruler and toothpick. Use a couple of pieces of thin cardboard or heavy paper (like grocery sack) to place on sides of each section as you sprinkle seived whites and yolks, alternately, over whole top.

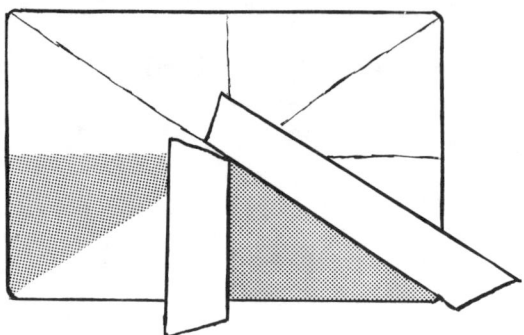

Stick small sprigs of parsley in rows between each section, then around all sides of salad. Sprinkle a narrow line of paprika down center of each section. Hold shaker on side (not straight up) to do this. Move shaker back and forth (lengthwise) along center of section.

VARIATION ON THE PRECEDING DESIGN.....

Make a similar design on the salad in a large, round bowl, using the same technique to make stripes with seived egg yolks and whites.

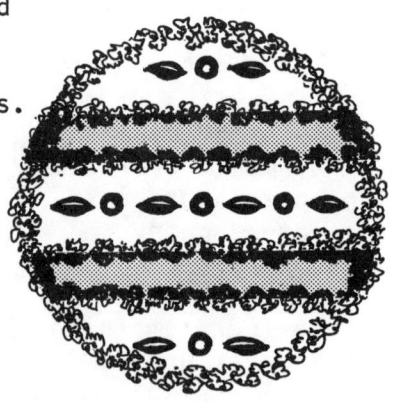

Decorate down centers of white stripes with slices of black olives and ovals of pimientoes, cut out with aspic cutters.

Fill in between stripes and around edge with small parsley sprigs.

AND ANOTHER VARIATION.....

Decorate this dish of potato salad with seived egg yolks and whites also, using a pattern and stencil this time to create a different design.

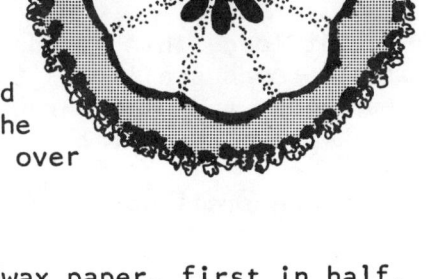

Before making the design, make sure the potato salad is smooth on top. (Rub the back of a large spoon all over the surface.)

Fold a 12" square of wax paper, first in half, then fourths, then into a triangle. Cut a scallop across the fold as shown below, approximately $3\frac{1}{2}$" from tip of triangle to highest point of scallop.

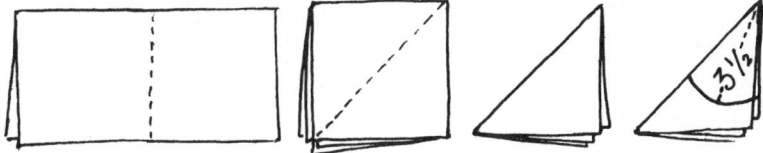

You now have pattern (A) and stencil (B).

Flatten out the creases as much as possible.

Set Pattern A down in the center of the dish of potato salad. Hold in place lightly with one hand while sprinkling seived egg yolks over the area outside of pattern. Remove pattern by lifting straight up.

Place Stencil B down on salad, making sure scallops match scalloped edge of egg yolks. Sprinkle seived egg whites all over area not covered by stencil, then remove stencil by lifting straight up.

Sprinkle narrow lines of paprika across center, from scallop to scallop.

Cut long, thin strips from whole pimientoes and place around scallops. Cut eight petal shapes from pimientoes and place around center, then set one black olive in center of petals.

Place small sprigs of parsley all around edge.

MEAT & CHEESE TRAYS

There's no limit to the designs that can be made when arranging meat and cheese on trays. Whether you plan a tray with all meat, all cheese or a combination of both, a symetrical design makes a most attractive arrangement. In other words, divide the tray into equal sections with different varieties of meat and/or cheese.

Meat and cheese slices can be placed flat on the tray in rows, with a few meat slices rolled up, then spaces filled in with sprigs of parsley and black olives.

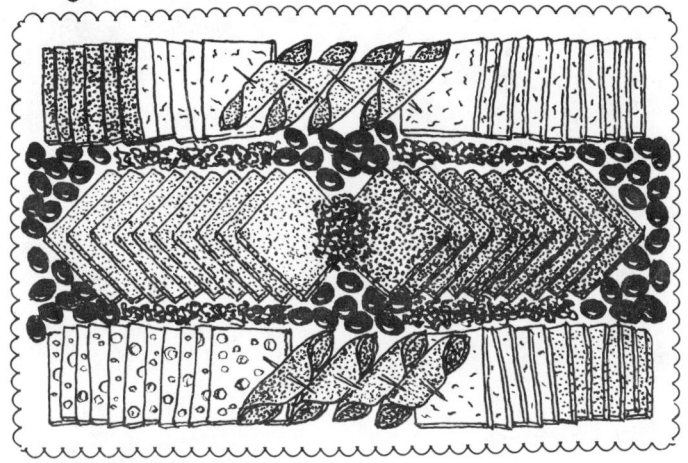

Or, meat slices can be rolled into cone shapes, & cheese slices placed flat in uniform sections on the tray.

Fill in spaces between sections with small sprigs of parsley.

Here is a tray with a combination of shrimp and cheese cubes.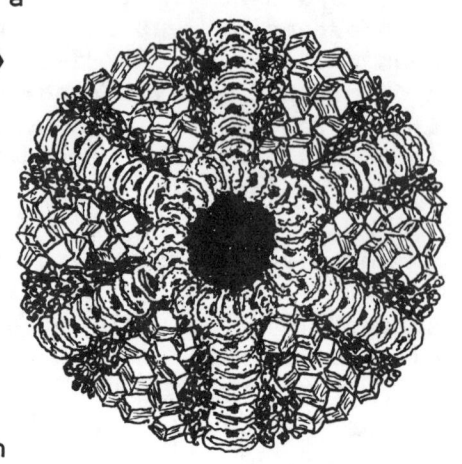

Place shrimp around edge of bowl of sauce in center, then lines of shrimp out to edge of tray.

Cut bulk cheese into 3/4" cubes and fill in spaces between lines of shrimp, then place parsley in between cheese and shrimp.

XI

MENUS

SHOWERS

Decorated Cake   Decorated Cake
Ice Cream   Punch
Coffee   Mints
o o o o o o o   o o o o o o o

Decorated Sandwich Loaf
Relishes
Beverage
Salted Nuts
o o o o o o o

TEAS

Tea Sandwiches   Canapes
Petits Fours   Miniature Pastries
Coffee & Tea   Coffee & Tea
Salted Nuts   Mints
o o o o o o o   o o o o o o o

CARD PARTIES

Individual Salad Molds
Asst. Crackers
Coffee & Tea
Salted Nuts
o o o o o o

Individual Dessert Molds
Cookies
Fruit Punch
o o o o o o

Canapes
Relishes
Beverages
o o o o o o

COCKTAIL PARTIES

Asst. Cold Hors d'Oeuvres
Mini Cheese Balls
Hot Mini Meat Balls
Cocktails
Salted Nuts
o o o o o o

Canapes
Deviled Eggs
Sm. Wheat Crackers
Stuffed Green Olives
Salted Nuts
Cocktails
o o o o o o

Asst. Hot Hors d'Oeuvres
Dips
Crackers & Chips
Cocktails
o o o o o o

BUFFETS

Chaud Froid Molds
Gelatine Salad Mold
Asst. Cheese Slices
Asst. Meat Slices
Variety Bread Slices
Relishes
Cake & Coffee
Champagne

o o o o o o

Sandwich Loaves
Party Logs (Meat)
Party Cheese Balls
Asst. Crackers
Deviled Eggs
Relishes
Coffee & Tea

o o o o o o

Fruit Jello Mold
Barbecued Pork Riblets
Cottage Cheese Salad
Cocktail Rye Bread
Relishes
Summer Coating Candies
Beverages

o o o o o o

 ## WEDDING RECEPTIONS

Punch
Wedding Cake
Mints
Salted Nuts
o o o o o o o

Champagne Punch
Wedding Cake
Hot & Cold Hors d'Oeuvres
Salted Nuts & Mints
o o o o o o o

Wedding Cake
Asst. Tea Sandwiches
Champagne or Fruit Punch
Salted Nuts & Mints
o o o o o o o

Asst. Cold Meats & Cheeses
Potato Salad
Asst. Variety Bread Slices
Relishes
Potato Chips
Wedding Cake
Fruit Punch
o o o o o o o

XII

══SERVINGS PER PERSON══

The quantity of food to be prepared for any occasion depends upon several factors: the occasion itself, the time of day, the age and sex of guests (young, old, all men, all women, etc.).

Exact requirements will vary. For example, a cocktail party with hors d'oeuvres <u>only</u> will require more per person than would be served with cocktails preceding a buffet supper, sit-down dinner, etc. Or, the hostess of a tea may wish to serve only sweets, in which case, they should be served in larger quantities than for a tea at which sandwiches <u>and</u> sweets are served.

The information on the next few pages should provide you with a basis on which to plan the amount of food to be prepared for a particular number of guests.

APPETIZERS

When hors d'oeuvres are to be served, the following suggested amounts are considered generous servings:

a. Cocktail party, regardless of starting time... 10 per guest.

b. Cocktails served before buffet luncheon... 2 per guest.

c. Cocktail hour, to be followed by buffet supper or sitdown dinner...4 per guest.

d. Wedding reception, if no other food except wedding cake...8 per guest.

e. For most other occasions, about 4 per guest per hour for the first two hours and two per hour after that.

NOTE: The above data on serving hors d'oeuvres also applies to canapes.

TEA SANDWICHES/PETITS FOURS/PASTRIES

For teas, showers, or other occasions when sweets and/or tea sandwiches are served:

Allow per person:

    Tea sandwiches--------3
    (4 for wedding reception if only cake is served.)

    Petit Fours------------2

    Miniature pastries-----1

MOLDS/SANDWICH LOAVES/PARTY LOGS

For a buffet, where many dishes are served, suggested serving for large molded dishes...1 small serving per person per each type mold. (For example, some guests will take a regular size serving of one dish and nothing from another dish.) The same serving applies to sandwich loaves on a buffet table.

For party logs, balls and other shapes...2 servings per person. (If these are served as hors d'oeuvres or canapes, these 2 servings would be included in the amount suggested to be served with cocktails.)

"MEAT & POTATOES"

For a buffet where cold cuts are served, along with potato salad, figure approximately 4 oz. of meat and 4 oz. servings of salad for each guest. If the meat tray(s) includes some cheese slices, figure on 4 oz. of meat and cheese combined.

Figure on 3 slices of variety breads for each guest. (Some may use only two, others, four.)

MINTS

For receptions, teas, etc....two to three per person.

PUNCHES

For receptions when punch is the only beverage, figure two 5 oz. servings per person, except in hot weather...then three to four per person.

NUTS

For cocktail parties...1 oz. (1/4 cup) per person. Other occasions...1/2 oz. (1/8 cup) per person.

There's Money in Catering & Decorating

If you enjoy catering enough to do it as a profitable side-line or full-time business, there are two books you should not be without.

One is "<u>How to Make Money in Cake Decorating: Owning & Operating a Successful Business in Your Home</u>". It is an extremely valuable publication which offers a wealth of information applicable to catering.

(You need to know nothing about cake decorating to understand the business basics of this remarkable book.)

Operating your own business today is so much more satisfying--emotionally and financially--than working for someone else, especially considering the many tax benefits you can enjoy. But you can also make money having just a <u>part-time</u> business while still working for others.

The second book is my own "<u>How to Make a Wedding Cake</u>". If you're supplying food to parties and receptions, why not go a step further and do wedding cakes? Weddings are <u>very</u> lucrative.

(For full details on these two books,
see the following pages.)

<u>A NOTE TO NON-DECORATORS:</u> "How to Make a Wedding Cake" is written for the person who already knows <u>how</u> to decorate. If you've had no previous cake decorating experience, may I suggest you enroll in the beginner's class in your community?

Classes are usually held in cake & food decorating supply stores and they are also taught through Adult Education courses. And if your town is large enough, the local Penney's or Ward's stores may also sponsor decorating classes. (Look in the Yellow Pages under "Cake Decorating Stores" or "Baker's Supplies" for the store/school nearest you.)

"BOOK OF THE YEAR"
Newsletter/Journal of American Cake Decorating

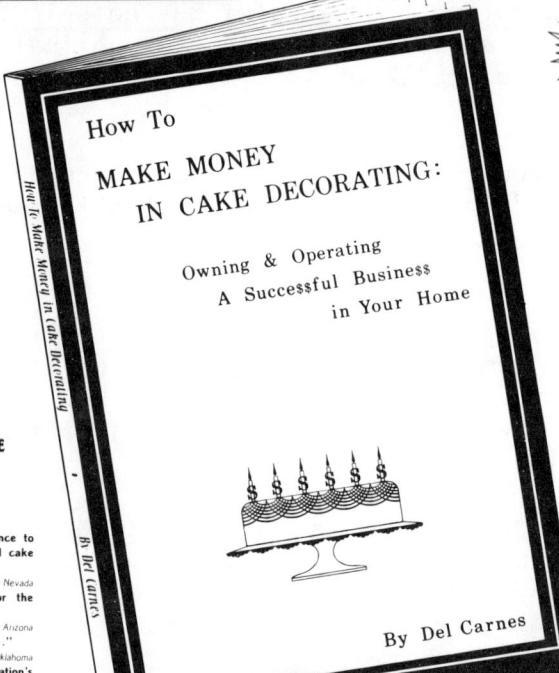

WHAT PEOPLE ARE SAYING ABOUT THIS BOOK

"An invaluable reference to those in the decorated cake business..."
Phyllis Holsey, Boulder City, Nevada

"It's must reading for the decorator/baker..."
Bernard Vest, Mesa, Arizona

"Worth every penny..."
Mrs. Keith Brandon, Edmond, Oklahoma

"Del Carnes is the nation's foremost authority on making money in Cake Decorating..."
Jim Maroney, Littleton, Colorado

"Very easy to read and understand. Book is so enthusiastic, it makes you want to start a business right away..."
Mrs. Jerry Thomas, Green River, Wyoming

6 x 9 Size
192 Pages with Index
14 Big Sections
Forms for Cake Orders, Deposits, Bookkeeping
Easy-to-wipe-clean soft cover

- Pricing Cakes
- Licenses & Permits
- Equipment & Supplies
- Tax Benefits
- Getting Customers
- Inexpensive Advertising
- Sample Order Forms

MORE MONEY-MAKING SECRETS →

The First Book Devoted Exclusively To This Important Subject!

- What you should know about advertising (newspapers, radio, TV, yellow pages).
- How to save on your labor costs.
- How you can avoid taxes — LEGALLY (and still keep the IRS happy).
- Simplified bookkeeping methods.
- Fringe benefits of your own business.
- How to stop customers from cancelling orders.
- You can work either full-time or part-time.

170

"HOW TO MAKE MONEY IN CAKE DECORATING:
OWNING & OPERATING A SUCCESSFUL BUSINESS IN YOUR HOME"

Thousands of Dollars of Essential Information that Took Years to Compile. NOW . . . available for YOU!!

DISCOVER

- How to start out with little or no investment.
- Three "magic" words to boost your sales.
- How to make sure you get paid.
- Secrets of discount buying.
- Importance of choosing a good name.
- How to save on supplies & ingredients
- How to donate to a charity and get a customer at the same time.
- How your business can survive when others around you are failing.
- . . . and MUCH, MUCH MORE!!!

YOU SHOULD BUY THIS BOOK . . .

IF
- You want to turn your "hobby" into a profitable home venture.
- You're an established decorator wanting to increase your sales.
- You're considering a career in Cake Decorating
- You're currently in business and need more vital information.
- You want to cope with inflation by using your decorating skills.

BECOME FINANCIALLY INDEPENDENT THROUGH CAKE DECORATING

For publication of this magnitude, with the wealth of profitable information it discloses, you'd expect to pay upwards of $25.00 . . .

BUT . . . "HOW TO MAKE MONEY IN CAKE DECORATING" is ONLY **$9.95**
(plus a small shipping/handling fee.)

Send for your No-Risk Trial Copy NOW . . . and get started on a Profitable Course of ACTION!!

ABOUT THE AUTHOR

Before he entered the Cake Decorating business, Del Carnes was a professional journalist, working for the Denver Post, Wichita Beacon, Wall Street Journal, and Variety, the show business paper. He joined the Mrs. Mayo's Company in the 1970's and helped make it one of the largest dealers of Cake Decorating supplies in the country, eventually establishing five stores with multi-million dollar gross sales. More recently, he has been devoting his time writing about the business side of Cake & Food Decorating.

"HOW TO MAKE MONEY IN CAKE DECORATING:
Owner & Operating a Successful Business in Your Home"
is sold at leading Cake & Food Decorating Supply Shoppes.
If your local store does not have the book,
or if it is not available at your favorite mail order house
you may write to:

Deco-Press Publishing Co.
Box 29489-CF
Denver, Colorado 80229

Please enclose payment of $11.45
($9.95 + shipping/handling charge of $1.50)
Price subject to change without notice.

MONEY-BACK GUARANTEE NO RISK TO YOU!

We make this Unconditional Promise. If "How to Make Money in Cake Decorating" is not what you thought it would be or if you are not completely satisfied — just return it within 30 days in as good a condition as you received it — and we will refund your money IMMEDIATELY. No questions asked!

NOTE: This book does not teach you how to decorate. Publisher presumes reader has decorating knowledge.

171

NOW ... for the FIRST TIME ... In ONE BOOK ...
Everything you always wanted to know about Wedding Cakes...!

"How to Make a Wedding Cake"

- How to Bake Them
- How to Assemble Them
- How to Cut Them
- How to Figure Yields
- How to Figure Batter Needed
- How Much Icing to Make
- How to Deliver Them Safely
- How to Price Them
- How to Advertise Them
- and Much More!

This fabulous publication has
15 Big Chapters
158 Pages
65 Illustrations
30 Charts, Graphs, Forms & Recipes
Revised & enlarged soft cover edition

Esther Murphy, the author, takes you from the breaking of the first egg for the batter through the completed cake on the reception table ... and along the way, she reveals all the information compiled in a lifetime of Decorating!!!!

Your Own Reference Library!
What Esther has taught thousands of students is now available in a **Single Source**. The information is at your fingertips!

Some of the information heretofore has been available only by searching through numerous publications. And much of it has never been available before!

Even if you are a Professional Decorator who has made hundreds of cakes, you'll discover **Ideas & Secrets** you never knew before!

Having the book is like having Esther in your own kitchen, helping you every step of the way:

Esther will show you:
- How to pre-plan your cake
- How to figure exact materials needed
- Secrets for making excellent batter
- 5 easy steps to icing cakes
- How to adjust for altitude
- Tips for Successful Baking
- Easy ways to figure amount of icing needed
- Step-by-step procedures for assembling cake
- How to box cakes & prepare them for safe delivery
- And a great deal more!

For the person in the Business of Cake Decorating
The Book Reveals

- Fool proof ways to price your cakes
- Methods of establishing market value
- Ways to understand costs
- Why deposits are important
- How to reduce & even stop last minute cancellations
- When you should deliver, and how
- Inexpensive ways to advertise
- Simple & easy promotion methods to increase business

Only $8.95
plus small shipping/handling charge

ABOUT THE AUTHOR

Esther Murphy has had a long & distinguished career in Cake Decorating as a teacher & author. She is the author of "The Art of Creative Cake Decorating"; "Holiday & Party Cakes"; "Mrs. Mayo's Book of Creative Foods".

NOTE: This book does not teach you how to decorate. Publisher presumes reader has decorating knowledge.

OTHER BENEFITS

The book includes

☐ Wedding Anniversaries from the First through the 60th with suggested gifts for each one

☐ Appropriate jewels for each month of the year

☐ Appropriate flowers for each month of the year

WHO SHOULD BUY THIS BOOK?

- Professional Decorators
- Commercial Bakers
- Caterers
- Cake Shoppe Owners
- Decorating Teachers
- Decorating Schools
  (Ideal textbook for Wedding Course)
- Student Decorators
- Bridal Shoppe Owners
- Wedding Consultants
- Non-professional Decorators (doing cakes for family, friends)
- Mothers of the Bride (who want to insure the cake is being done properly)
- Anyone who has ever thought about putting a Wedding Cake together

AND

Decorators who want to cash in on the **MULTI-MILLION $$ WEDDING CAKE BUSINESS!**

What Others say about "How to Make a Wedding Cake"

"... It's the foremost book on constructing a Wedding Cake. Whether you are decorating for pleasure or profit, making a cake for your daughter or a friend, you shouldn't be without this book. **Dozens** of shortcuts and secrets published for the first time. An invaluable publication you'll treasure all your life."
(Deco-Press Publishers)

"... Have you wondered how to price a cake, how to advertise, how to assemble, or cut a Wedding Cake? In her book, which is prepared to answer just such questions, Esther Murphy gives you the practical approach, aided by many, many sketches, and line drawings ... Even one hint gained from this book could make **all** the difference!"
(Maid of Scandinavia)

"... It is very well done and provides much valuable information not available otherwise ..."
(Mildred Brand, Country Kitchen, Fort Wayne, Indiana)

"... a Fabulous book. Not to be missed ..."
(Zella Skinner - Miller, South Dakota)

No-Risk, Money-Back Guarantee

We make this Unconditional Guarantee: If, within 30 days, you are not completely satisfied — if this book is not what you thought it was — just return it in as good condition as you received it — and we will refund your money! No questions asked.

"HOW TO MAKE A WEDDING CAKE" is sold at leading Cake & Food Decorating Supply Shoppes. If your local store does not have the book, or if it is not available at your favorite mail order house, you may write to:

Deco-Press Publishing Co.
Box 29489-CF
Denver, Colorado 80229

Please enclose payment of $10.45
($8.95 + shipping/handling charge of $1.50)
Price subject to change without notice.

About the Author

Esther Murphy is one of the pioneers of American Cake Decorating. Long before the current crop of books appeared on the scene, Esther wrote and illustrated the two best-selling decorating books of the day----"The Art of Creative Cake Decorating" and "Holiday and Party Cakes".

Although those publications are out of print today, they have become collector's items, much sought after by decorators.

Many successful and talented cake decorators throughout the country today are either former students of Esther's or cut their decorating teeth on her books. She is known and admired by thousands of decorators.

Since the early 1970's, she has been chief designer and teacher for the Mrs. Mayo's Company.

In addition to the "Book of Creative Foods", she also is the author of the best-selling "How to Make a Wedding Cake".

She lives and works in Denver, Colorado.